A HOPE DEFERRED

A COUPLE'S GUIDE TO COPING WITH INFERTILITY

JILL BAUGHAN

MULTNOMAH
Portland, Oregon 97266

D1472652

Unless otherwise noted, all Scripture references are from the New American Standard Bible, © The Lockman Foundation 1960, 1962, 1963, 1968, 1971, 1972, 1973, 1975, 1977.

Scripture references marked TLB are from The Living Bible, © 1971 by Tyndale House Publishers.

Scripture references marked NEB are from the New English Bible, © 1961, 1970 by the Delegates of the Oxford University Press and the Syndics of the Cambridge University Press.

A HOPE DEFERRED
© Multnomah Press
Portland, Oregon 97266

Multnomah Press is a ministry of Multnomah School of the Bible, 8435 NE Glisan Street, Portland, Oregon 97220.

Printed in the United States of America

All rights reserved. No part of this publication may be reproduced, stored in a retrieval system, or transmitted, in any form or by any means, electronic, mechanical, photocopying, recording, or otherwise, without the prior written permission of the publisher.

Library of Congress Cataloging-in-Publication-Data

Baughan, Jill.
    A hope deferred : a couples' guide to coping with infertility / Jill Baughan.
      p.   cm.
    Bibliography: p.
    ISBN 0-88070-303-2
    1. Infertility—Popular works.   2. Christian life—1960-
I.Title.
RC889.B38   1989
616.6'92—dc20
                                 89-32519
                                     CIP

89 90 91 92 93 94 95 96 97 98 - 10 9 8 7 6 5 4 3 2 1

For Ben

Contents

Acknowledgments

One big hug for Deena Davis and Jane Aldrich Brown of Multnomah Press . . . Your support and belief in the value of this book mean more to me than you'll ever know.

Diane Ager . . . From the very beginning your prayers have pulled me out of the muck many times.

Mark Booth . . . My teacher, encourager, and friend. No matter how far away you move, you'll always have a special place in my heart.

My parents-in-law, Arlene and Arthur Baughan . . . Thank you for taking the time and tears to show your son how to be a real man—and then sharing him with me.

My mom, Mary Ellis . . . More than anyone else, you have taught me by your example that happiness really is a choice.

Ben . . . The love of my life. You're the best!

And one extra-big hug for Jamie . . . My joy in the morning.

Part One:
In The Beginning

I just can't believe it. All those years I took birth control pills for nothing. I thought we were so normal. This is something that always happens to somebody else. . . .

It starts out simply enough. For me, it was a phone call at work from my doctor.

"Mrs. Baughan, we have a problem here." *Understatement of the year.* "But we may be able to help you and your husband." *Famous last words.*

Almost always the news comes as a shock. You've dreamed of the family you would have some day. You have tried without success to conceive and are now classed as infertility patients. You are surprised . . . confused . . . worried . . . afraid.

It takes some time to get used to the idea, to admit even to yourselves that you are infertile. Part One of this book can help you adjust and find answers to other people's questions as well as your own. The following pages also offer suggestions on surviving an investigation that seems to last forever.

Yes, you have a problem--but you also have a great God to help you accept it, live with it, and grow from it.

I ran into Julie today, and she made me sorry I ever told her about our infertility.

"Oh, Jill," she teased, "you know the surest way to get pregnant, don't you?"

I cringed, praying that she wouldn't say what I've heard too many times before.

"Just adopt a baby! Why, I know a girl . . ."

Dear God, if one more person opens one more mouth to give me one more piece of "expert" advice, I think I'll start telling people we never wanted kids anyway.

1

Misunderstandings

Drink lots of water."

"Take cough medicine."

"Quit jogging."

"Quit your job."

"Forget about it for a while."

"Take a vacation."

"There must be some unconfessed sin in your life. Find it and get right with God."

"You'd better adopt right now. If you never have kids, you'll end up bitter and self-centered."

"Have intercourse more often; take every chance you can get."

"Have intercourse less often; give the sperm time to build up."

"Have intercourse standing on your head."

"What?"

"I mean, after intercourse, stand on your head."

What ever happened to afterglow?

If you've experienced infertility, it's probably not hard for you to believe I was given all this advice at one time or another by well-meaning people who wanted to help when they discovered my husband and I were infertile. And just for the record, none of it worked.

Once your infertility is made public (or at least semi-private), you can expect much advice to roll your way. And when it does, it helps to be prepared—intellectually, emotionally, and spiritually—because much of what you hear will be outdated, out of context, and just plain out to lunch. In the past few years, I have spent a lot of time trying to separate myth from fact, religious thinking from spiritual truth. And I've found that few subjects are as loaded as the desire for and the inability to produce children: loaded with emotion, yes, and with misunderstandings. Here are a few you'll probably confront.

"Infertility is synonymous with sterility"

Look up the words *infertile* and *sterile* in the dictionary, and you'll find them listed as synonyms. Don't believe it; at least don't apply it to your own infertility. In terms of pregnancy, sterility is the permanent, irreversible inability to produce children. A woman with irreparable ovary damage is considered physically sterile. A man with an uncorrectable sperm count of zero is sterile. On the other hand, as obstetrician/gynecologist James Howard states, infertility is "a current condition—one that prevails at the present moment and prevents conception of children. A couple who is infertile today may be fertile tomorrow or next month or next year."[1]

In a way, permanence would make the condition easier to adjust to. I've often thought, "Lord, if I only knew I could never have a baby, then I could concentrate on other options. I could quit hoping and praying for pregnancy; I could quit setting myself up for an emotional landslide every month when my period comes. Then again, if only I knew that some day I'd get pregnant, I could wait a year, two, three, five, or even ten—if only I knew."

But none of us knows, and it's this uncertainty that keeps us in a maddening race, wanting to drop out, to stop, yet not wanting to diminish any faint hope of conceiving a child.

Sterile is final. Period.

Infertile is conditional, always followed by a question mark.

"Infertility is a rare condition"

Well, it feels like a rare condition when

> you visit the hospital's maternity ward and look through the glass at all those rows of warm, squirming bundles;

> your neighbor opens up and tells you how worried she is that she might be pregnant.

But the truth is, about one in six couples of childbearing age at any given time is infertile.[2] Statistically, that's sixteen such couples out of every hundred sitting in church with you on a given Sunday morning. Of course, it never seems that way. All you see is a church nursery full of someone else's babies.

It feels like a rare condition because we tend to isolate ourselves from the rest of the world. We shy away from talking about it because we (a) think no one will understand, (b) are embarrassed, or (c) we don't want people making assumptions about our sex life.

There seemed to be no end to the "When are you going to have a baby?" questions that church people were asking me. And at first, I was a little embarrassed to admit our problem. Then I wrote an article about infertility for a denominational magazine, and the month it came out I felt as if I'd been literally exposed in front of five hundred people. But to my surprise, many infertile couples (and formerly infertile ones) pulled me aside to talk about it, some for the first time.

We're not alone, we're not freaks of nature. And it helps to know that.

"Infertility is 'all in your head'"

In 1797, William Buchan concluded that "barrenness is often the consequence of grief, sudden fear, anxiety or any of the passions which tend to obstruct the mental flux."[3]

Exactly how often is "often?"

There's no doubt that psychological factors do play a part in a couple's inability to conceive. It never seemed to fail for us: on my peak fertility night we'd plan to get to bed early, but for one reason or another we would land on the mattress totally exhausted at the end of the day. Lying there, knowing what we ought to do, but not in the mood to do it, we'd look at each other, sigh . . . and usually do it anyway. But there were some nights when we just couldn't stand another evening of "duty sex," so we skipped it. Of course that ruined our chances for the month. Thus our frame of mind affected our fertility.

There are other ways psychology can affect fertility, one of the most common being stress. Joseph McFalls cites studies which indicate that psychic stress can reduce sperm production and lower the quality and quantity of sperm. He also notes studies which claim that stress can suppress egg production in women, "reduce the fertility of the ovum, cause dysfunction in tubal transport and alter cervical secretions" that may immobilize sperm.[4]

But how often? No one knows for sure. McFalls admits that the study of the effects of the mind on the ability to produce children is still in the beginning stages. He does point out that most of these conditions are treatable.

On the other hand, Robert Glass, professor of obstetrics and gynecology at the University of California Medical Center, and Ronald Ericsson, a research biologist, feel that "severe anxieties can interfere with ovulation or with the frequency of intercourse, and thus can cause infertility. Barring these physical problems, however, there is no evidence that anxieties about infertility actually cause infertility."[5]

There may be some good sense in the "relax, forget about it, take a vacation" advice. And, of course, people will have a pocketful of stories about how a couple they know adopted a child, and when the pressure was off— their attention focused on something besides infertility— the wife was pregnant a few months later. I don't doubt that these stories are true; I've heard plenty myself. It's just that there are many more cases of parents who adopt and don't get pregnant. Not a good way to cure infertility, to say the least.

About 90 percent of the time, doctors can find a physical cause for your childlessness. Before you conclude your infertility is psychogenic, it's important to undergo a thorough physical workup; and even if a specific cause can't be found, psychological factors aren't necessarily to blame. Ask your physician how these factors may be involved in your case.

"Infertility is punishment from God"

There must be some reason God is punishing you, you think. The search for an answer to the "why" of a fertility problem seems endless. We're answer-oriented people; when we can't logically explain our infertility, we search for a cause, any cause. And when we can't rationalize our way into an answer, we often pin the blame on ourselves. Our misfortune must be chastisement from God for some wrongdoing on our part. We begin to feel that if only we knew exactly what we were being punished for, we could correct it and get our baby.

How tempting it is for us as Christians to forget that we've been freed from the mistakes of our past. With the acceptance of Christ comes the gift of forgiveness, which allows us to stop bleeding and start healing. We may be experiencing the consequences of some bad judgments we have made, but it's important to remember that infertility is not a slap in the face from God. In her book *Beyond Heartache*, Mari Hanes explains that the law of human conception has been ordered by God just as the law of gravity and all other natural phenomena. Ideally, sperm meets egg and produces a healthy baby. "Yet," she says, "it is important to see that a young, unmarried girl who becomes pregnant has not been 'zapped' with a pregnancy from God. Instead, she has used the prerogative God gave her to begin a new life. Neither is God punishing you by keeping you from getting pregnant; something is interfering with the natural law of conception."[6]

"Woman's highest calling is to bear and rear children"

In 1940, my mother had to run away to get married—not because her parents disapproved (actually, her mother came along!) but because she was a school teacher. The ceremony was in July, so my parents lived apart for two months. When school began, they came out of hiding with a wedding announcement in the local newspaper. Why the big secret? Had the school board found out before September that she was married, they would have refused to renew her contract. Married women were bad risks; they just taught school to pass time till they could get pregnant and quit work. After all, that's basically what women are for, isn't it?

Even as late as the 1950s, psychiatrist Edward Strecker wrote, "The main function of woman is to give birth to children and make a home in which they may be reared. The function of men is to provide the means which makes it possible for woman to carry out her function." Double whammy—here's a blow to the infertile male's self-concept too. Strecker goes on to say that "history shows that the most successful races and nations have been those who for the most part were mothered by real women able to accept and enjoy their real function."[8]

That hurts. And even today, in many parts of the world, a woman is not fully accepted into a man's family until she has had a child—preferably a boy. In middle America we're still haunted by the notion that a woman's worth, at least in part, depends upon her ability to be a "real" woman and mother children.

I have a friend who had been trying to start a family for years. In casual conversation with an acquaintance, my friend admitted her childlessness (but not her infertility) to which the lady replied, "I can't believe you're selfish enough to be married so long and not have any children." Unfortunately, this is a common assumption people make about the childless or parents with only one child.

It's reassuring to know that Jesus' emphasis was on personhood. Vicky Love, in her book *Childless Is Not Less*, makes reference to the passage in Luke where a woman in the crowd calls to Jesus, "Blessed is the womb that bore You, and the breasts at which You nursed." Jesus replies, "On the contrary, blessed are those who hear the word of God, and observe it."[9] His answer reveals an interest not in a person's "true function," but in who that person is apart from the labels one could impose.

There is certainly nothing wrong with desiring motherhood. I do. In fact, there's everything right about it. There is something wrong, however, with the idea that reproduction equals worth. We must—as Christ did— examine the heart, not the hormones.

"Infertility is a woman's problem"

For many years this was thought to be true, basically because mankind lacked knowledge about the physical process of conception. Medical science, of course, has come a long way, and though we don't know everything about birth and conception, we're aware of many physical causes of infertility, some of which are attributable to men. In fact, Glass and Ericsson estimate that "40-50 percent of infertility is attributable wholly or in part to a problem in the male."[10]

It's sad that still there are doctors who will put the wife through a thorough medical investigation before simply asking the husband for a semen specimen. Equally disturbing is the number of men who refuse to have a semen analysis done for fear the results will somehow put a dent in their masculinity, though machismo is no relative of fertility.

For many, there is a curious stigma attached to the

attempt to correct a low sperm count. After a vari-ococelectomy, my husband was home in the backyard puttering around. A neighbor passing by, thinking that maybe a little humor would make him feel better, yelled (for the benefit of the rest of the neighborhood as well), "Hey Ben! How'd the sex change turn out?" Of course this did nothing to boost my husband's ego; yet he laughed it off, chalked it up to thoughtlessness, and went on work-ing. I was the one who ran to the house in tears.

Infertility, and all its excess emotional weight, is in reality a couple's problem. Viewed any other way, this crisis is bound to overload one partner with false guilt and anxiety. It is sure to create distance between husband and wife. To think of infertility as your problem or my problem is not only psychologically damaging, it's just plain ignorant.

"People—especially women—have an instinctive desire for children that must be fulfilled"

In the past, the desire for many children was practical as well as emotional. High infant mortality was one reason to reproduce as much as possible. Furthermore, in the days when families were largely self-sufficient, more children meant more physical help in growing food and sustaining life for the family. But now the infant mortality rate is lower in our country than it's ever been,[11] and most of us just hop into the car and go to the grocery store to sustain life.

So if not practical, is our desire for children instinc-tive? There are no studies to prove conclusively that the desire for children is completely innate. In part, we are nudged by our environment. Think about when your infertility hurts the most.

I had come a long way toward accepting our infertility; I was at peace with our status and my frustration with God had ebbed into acceptance. Then a good friend of mine announced that she was pregnant. All the anger, hurt, desperation, and urgency gripped me once again, and I was determined to get pregnant as quickly as possible. Poor Ben. I lit on him at every opportunity, believing that if we tried hard, fast, and often enough, we could make ourselves a baby. That was one wild month.

Of course, my period eventually came; I had to catch my breath and start all over again. I did learn one thing though: our surroundings have considerable effect on our desires.

This is not to say that our environment is solely responsible for "baby hunger." We can long for children when there's not a pregnant woman in sight. But there are people who insist that all women want to have babies and ought to, or that baby hunger comes as naturally to both sexes as the appetite for food. They say this yearning for children is a basic biological desire, and if it is not fulfilled by children, we are destined to spend our lives frustrated, incomplete, and bitter. Helene Deutsch even categorizes women who have been unable to master the "sterility trauma" by agreeing with the words of a Polish poet: "Feminine hearts are beehives: when the honey of maternal love does not fill them, they become vipers' nests."[12]

Of course there have been times when each of us has reacted to the frustration in pretty wicked ways. We are still affected by instincts and circumstances, but our response to our infertility—as to any other crisis—is our choice, not predestined by a biological drive.

When your head is filled to capacity with the alleged wisdom of others, there are times when you want to scream "Shut up!" to the entire world so you can hear and feel the real truth about your infertility.

And how do you find that truth? Through doctors, yes, and books too. But the heart of our search should be with God himself, as we strain to distinguish his voice from all others, as we continually reach for a closer relationship with him. He tells us what he wants us to know, sometimes bit by bit and much too slowly (according to our timetables). But in a close partnership with God is a peculiar kind of liberation—from anxiety and fear, and from the wrongheaded ideas of many well-meaning people.

> *"If you abide in My word, then you are truly disciples of Mine;*
> *and you shall know the truth, and the truth shall make you free"*
> (John 8:31-32).

Chapter 1, Notes

1. James T. Howard and Dodi Schultz, *We Want to Have a Baby* (New York: E.P. Dutton, 1979), 2.

2. Gerhard Bettendorf, "The Normal Infertile Couple," *Infertility: Male and Female*, ed. Vaclav Insler and Bruno Lunenfeld (New York: Churchill Livingstone, 1986), 333.

3. Virginia Adams, "The Odds of Psychosomatic Childlessness," *Psychology Today*, May 1980, 33.

4. Joseph A. McFalls, Jr., *Psychopathology and Subfecundity* (New York: Academic Press, 1979), 58-64.

5. Robert Glass and Ronald J. Ericsson, *Getting Pregnant in the 1980s* (Berkeley: University of California Press, 1982), 4.

6. Mari Hanes with Jack Hayford, *Beyond Heartache* (Wheaton, Ill.: Tyndale House Publishers, 1984), 89.

7. Edward Strecker and Vincent T. Lathbury, *Their Mothers' Daughters* (New York: Lippincott, 1956), 13.

8. Ibid.

9. Luke 11:28

10. Glass and Ericsson, *Getting Pregnant*, 37.

11. In the United States in 1918, approximately one infant in ten (live births) died before the age of twelve months. In 1985, approximately one infant in one hundred died before the age of twelve months. *Statistical Abstract of the United States*, U.S. Department of Commerce (Bureau of Foreign and Domestic Commerce) no. 48 (1925), 80; no. 108 (1988), 76.

12. Helene Deutsch, *The Psychology of Women: Motherhood*, vol. 2 (New York: Grune and Stratton, 1945), 169.

I feel so alone as I walk down the hospital corridor to X-ray. I am told to strip down from the waist, put on the gray hospital gown and wait awhile. My heart beats faster. Finally, I am ushered into the X-ray room. I lie on the table; they take a few pictures. Enter the doctor: fortyish, balding, mustachioed, quiet, and very Irish. Under any other circumstances, I would be totally charmed. Today, however, I just want to get this over with. I try to breath deeply and relax. It's hard to relax with both feet in the air. I glance at the doctor's ammunition: the speculum, the long tweezers and other unidentified hardware—all used for a set of very uncomfortable preliminaries. Cramps. Now they're pulling out the TV screen. The doctor puts on an asbestos apron. (Is this safe?) His nurse helps him fill the syringe with dye. He crouches down into the firing position. Get an angle on my pelvis. Ready? Shoot.

Oh Lord, this better be worth it. . .

2

So What's the Matter?

I read somewhere that a thorough investigation of infertility will take two to three months. That may be true if
everything goes perfectly—if nobody goes on vacation at
the wrong time; if the lab equipment and testing methods
don't break down; if no one gets sick; and if your body
cooperates. Sometimes it takes three months, sometimes it
takes three years. One thing is for sure: it always takes too
long.

If you've considered yourself reasonably healthy to this
point, so many trips to the doctor's office can be quite
disturbing. You may feel as though you body isn't yours
any more; pieces of it are on slides, in petri dishes, under
microscopes, sent off to labs and deposited in specimen
cups. You feel poked, prodded, pained, and very much out
of control.

I've found that the best way to cope with these stressful emotions during the investigation is to arm yourself
with knowledge—knowledge about the procedures your
doctor suggests and, just as important, knowledge about
the workings of your own system. In order to comprehend
and minimize your fears about tests and treatments, it's

helpful to have a basic understanding of how our bodies are supposed to be operating.

The Female

A woman is born with all the eggs she will ever produce. Each month, at the beginning of her cycle, the pituitary gland puts out FSH (follicle-stimulating hormone) which stimulates the growth and maturity of the follicle—a sticky substance surrounding the maturing egg. Around the middle of the month, this follicle begins to produce estrogen which (1) builds up the uterine lining in preparation for pregnancy; (2) opens the cervix; (3) readies the cervical mucus, making it thin, watery, and easy for sperm to penetrate; and (4) tells the pituitary gland to start producing LH (luteinizing hormone). The release of LH weakens the wall of the follicle so the egg can escape the follicle, then the ovary. This is ovulation. Now, instead of producing estrogen as it did before, the follicle (left behind in the ovary) changes faces. It turns yellow, becoming the corpus luteum ("yellow body") and begins to produce progesterone. The progesterone (1) causes the midcycle rise in the basal body temperature, (2) closes the cervix, (3) changes the consistency of the cervical mucus to thick, sticky, and difficult for sperm to penetrate; and (4) prepares the uterine lining for implantation.

The released egg is then picked up by the fimbria, fingerlike structures at the end of the fallopian tubes, and pulled through one of the tubes by the beating of tiny hairs on the fimbria and muscular action of the tube.

The Male

Meanwhile, in the male, the pituitary gland stimulates the production of LH (which initiates the production of testosterone, the hormone responsible for male characteristics and sex drive) and FSH (which encourages sperm production). A man is not born with all the sperm he will ever have, however. At puberty the testicles begin a continuous process of manufacturing millions of them, but each sperm cell takes about sixty to ninety days to develop to maturity. So, though the testicles are prolific, they won't be rushed. When the sperm are ready, they journey through a series of winding "roads" through a man's body.

> Out of the testis, through the epididymis, they begin the long haul upstream through the vas deferens. Passing before the pubic bone, they head inward over the bladder and finally down to the seminal vesicle where they get to rest while waiting for the go-ahead. They gather in joyous anticipation of the big send-off. At last the signal comes and, like lemmings to the sea, millions upon millions swarm through the prostate where they are reinforced with more fluid, pumped down the urethra, and with a final surge, forced out through the penis to the great beyond.[1]

And what happens in "the great beyond"? Only a fraction of the sperm ejaculated make it through the unfriendly, acidic environment of the vagina to travel through the cervix and uterus, then up to the fallopian tubes where the egg waits. Sometimes the sperm fertilizes the egg. But when no fertilized egg travels to the uterus and implants in the prepared lining, the corpus luteum stops producing progesterone, the lining is shed in menstruation, and the whole cycle begins again—a cycle very familiar to you.

Even from just a short description of how our bodies work, it's easy to see how delicate is the balance of mechanics and hormones, and how an imbalance could prevent conception. Thus, a basic workup to check out your system is usually the first part of an infertility investigation.

The Basic Workup

If possible, try to see the doctor together, particularly on the first visit. The support of your spouse can be a big comfort, and you both need to hear what the doctor has to say. Remember, infertility is a couple's problem that requires physical and emotional cooperation from both partners. Each of you will need to give specific information to the doctor and assistance to each other, especially in the beginning.

Medical History

In the consultation, the doctor will ask both of you questions about your medical past. For women, these questions concern your menstrual history: How old were you when your periods started? How long do you menstruate? Do you experience painful cramps during your period? There will also be questions about your medical history concerning surgeries, past pregnancies, miscarriages, terminated pregnancies, prior vaginal or pelvic examinations. A man will be asked many questions about childhood illnesses, any infections or present illnesses, adult mumps, previous surgery or injury, and his use of alcohol or drugs.

This feels like playing Twenty Questions, but your answers contain information your doctor must know in order to help you. On your first visit, make sure your doctor has all available records that might have any bearing on your fertility.

Sexual History

For this information, the doctor will ask both of you questions about your sex life: the frequency, timing, and technique of intercourse; use of birth control, douches and lubricants; any discomfort you experience during inter-course and whether ejaculation takes place.

Yes, these are very personal matters—questions you've probably never had to answer before. But it is important that you be 100 percent honest in answering them, even if you feel uncomfortable doing so. If you only have inter-course once a year on Columbus Day, say so. The doctor needs this information to help you become parents, not to pry into your private life. And most professionals who must ask these questions have seen and heard it all before, so you needn't worry about shocking the doctor. Physi-cians who work with infertility patients realize that no couple leads a charmed sex life.

Physical Examination

A woman's doctor will generally do a Pap smear and give her a pelvic exam to check organs such as her uterus, vagina, ovaries, and cervix for abnormalities, and to look for signs of pelvic infection. The doctor will also examine her body for breast development, acne, signs of hirsutism (hairiness), and weight (both over and under).

A man will have his scrotum examined for testicular size and shape, a varicocele, or undescended testicles. His doctor (usually a urologist) will also take note of his distribution of hair and fat, and will examine the prostate gland through his rectum.

Blood tests on the man and woman may also be done to check for metabolic or hormonal problems that may be contributing to infertility.

Both you and your spouse should be examined thor-oughly, even if there is an obvious cause for infertility in one partner, since infertility for so many couples is a result of combined factors.

Basal Body Temperature

Early in the investigation, your doctor will probably ask you to take your basal body temperature each morning and record it on a special chart. Since the rise and fall of your temperature often reflects your body's response to ovarian hormones, the BBT chart can give the doctor a clue to any of several problems you might have.

Typically, the first day of menstruation is Day 1 on the chart. Around midcycle, progesterone production causes the temperature to rise, indicating ovulation. Close to the end of the cycle, if you are not pregnant, progesterone production stops, and your temperature begins to fall—an indication your period is on its way.

Charting your temperature sounds simple and painless, and actually it is at first. After a while, however, you might find yourself obsessed with the rise and fall of your temperature, and when it begins to fall, it can ruin your day before it even starts. When my temperature dropped, denial of the inevitable usually set in. Ben and I could think of a dozen reasons why that drop couldn't mean my period was coming: the room was too cold that night (it usually *was* cold, but the thermometer didn't know that); it was a bad thermometer (we always had three or four on hand to act as "control" thermometers); or I didn't leave it in my mouth long enough (fifteen minutes isn't long enough?).

Furthermore, the mechanics of taking it every morning before you even go to the bathroom, sit up, or blink can be pretty irritating after a while.

To help make the task a little more pleasant, try making the process a joint effort. It's nice if the husband will get the thermometer for his wife, then use those couple of minutes for cuddling instead of jumping out of bed or going back to sleep. Granted, she may not feel too romantic with a stick poking out of her mouth, but it can be a nice time to hold each other. Then if he will record her temperature, the process will become a shared event.

If you're ovulating regularly, sometimes you can narrow your temperature-taking to a ten-day range around ovulation, but you need to check with your doctor first.

One other problem with the BBT chart involves the little squares designed for your arrows, Xs, or Os that indicate when you've had intercourse. Recording your sex life on paper is threatening to many people, and there's hardly an infertile couple who, upon seeing only one X in the last two or three weeks, hasn't been tempted to insert a few more in strategic spots before the doctor looks at the chart. But the doctor is concerned about how your schedule of intercourse affects your fertility, not whether you're coupling according to the national average, so do be honest about it.

Post-Coital Test (Sims-Huhner Test)

The post-coital test helps the doctor evaluate the quality of the woman's cervical mucus around the time of ovulation when it should be thin and stretchy, and thus receptive to sperm (an indication that estrogen is present). It can also help the doctor evaluate sperm survival in the mucus.

At an infertility seminar I attended not long ago, a gynecologist referred to this one as an "easy test." I had to laugh. Easy for him maybe, but not always for his patients.

The test must be scheduled a day or two before ovulation. During that time, the couple makes an appointment with the doctor and has intercourse, usually within a couple of hours before the appointment. At the office, the doctor takes a sample of the cervical mucus and looks at it under a slide to check for lively, motile sperm. It is no more uncomfortable than a pelvic exam, and some couples are actually able to make a game of it. However, for many people, this arrangement can be, as one fellow put it, "the worst sex you will ever have." I've always felt particularly sorry for a man in this case, since he is so pressured to "produce" right down to the hour. If he cannot, he feels he has wasted an entire month and must wait four more weeks until his wife's mucus is receptive to sperm again.

If this is a problem for you, there are a couple things you can do to help yourself. If you're not morning people, try not to schedule yourselves for an 8:30 A.M. appointment. If you must, however, some doctors will let you have intercourse the night before, even though quite a bit of time may elapse between intercourse and appointment.

Finally, remember that there are usually a couple of days when a woman's cervical mucus is thin, so chances are if you're unsuccessful the first time, you can reschedule the appointment for a few hours later, or even the next day.

Specialized Tests

In a group discussion at a meeting I attended, one woman told of her husband's support at her hysterosalpingogram (I'll explain this test in a moment). He kept saying, "You're not alone, we're in this together." But she had been under so much physical stress, she blurted out, "Oh yeah? Where are they gonna shoot your dye?"

"I felt so bad after I said that," she admitted later.

It's tough on whomever happens to be going through testing at the moment. Psychologically you can share the burden, but physically it's only one person at a time who's hurting, and this can be a lonely experience.

To help yourself during these specialized tests, do be aware of exactly what test is being performed, why it's necessary, and what the results may be. Knowing what to expect can allay some of your apprehension. Also, verbalizing your fears (and encouraging your spouse to do the same) can take some of the weight off your shoulders at this time.

Tests for Her

Hysterosalpingogram. This mouthful of a word is an X-ray, usually performed a few days after the menstrual flow has stopped, which helps the doctor determine whether the fallopian tubes are blocked and whether the uterus is shaped normally.

To undergo this procedure, the patient lies on an examining table while a radio opaque dye is squirted through a syringe into the uterus and fallopian tubes until they are full. If the liquid flows smoothly through the uterus and tubes and out into the abdomen, this generally indicates there is no obstruction.

This is not a foolproof test, though. Spasms in the tubes can prevent dye from flowing through. Furthermore, the test gives no information about the condition of the ovaries or the outer surfaces of the tubes where adhesions may form.

The procedure can be pretty uncomfortable; dilation of the cervix and application of the dye generally cause cramps. Because of this, some doctors recommend sedatives or a paracervical block before beginning the process.

Endometrial biopsy. The endometrial biopsy is helpful in determining whether or not ovulation has occurred. In this procedure, the physician inserts a speculum into the vagina, then a clamp to hold the cervix in place. A thin tube is then used to scrape off a sample of the uterine lining. The sample is usually sent to a lab for endometrial dating. Here a pathologist can examine the tissue and estimate what day of the cycle the sample was taken. If the lab's day and the day on your temperature chart correspond, chances are you have produced sufficient amounts of estrogen and progesterone to ovulate and prepare the uterus for implantation of a fertilized egg.

All this may cause some pinching and cramping during the process, and some women experience some bleeding and minor cramps afterward. However, the procedure only takes a few minutes.

Laparoscopy. A laparoscopy is minor surgery, usually performed under general anesthesia. The surgeon inserts a small lighted telescope into a tiny incision (about a quarter of an inch) in the abdomen, right around the navel. This enables the doctor to see the internal organs and check for endometriosis or scar tissue that may have formed around tubes and ovaries and could interfere with egg pickup and delivery.

Some problems are not only seen but are corrected during the laparoscopy. Through a second incision made in the lower abdomen, minor adhesions can often be cut, and mild endometriosis can be treated by electrocautery or laser surgery. For this reason, laparoscopy often eliminates the need for major surgery.

Normally the procedure is performed on an outpatient basis. Afterward, there is some abdominal pain due to the incision, and shoulder pain due to the carbon dioxide gas used during surgery. All this should subside in a couple of days.

Hysteroscopy. Sometimes the hysterosalpingogram will show abnormalities within the uterus. If this is the case, a hysteroscopy may be in order.

With a hysteroscope (a small instrument with a fiber optic lens) inserted through the vagina and cervix, a doctor can see inside the uterus and even correct some problems. For example, the doctor can remove polyps or cut through scar tissue and possibly eliminate the need for major surgery.

This procedure can be done either in the hospital or doctor's office under general or local anesthesia. It may cause some cramping similar to the discomfort that accompanies a hysterosalpingogram.

Tests for Him

Semen analysis. A vital component of a complete infertility examination is the man's contribution of a semen sample, analyzed for three main factors: sperm count (the number of sperm per cubic centimeter or milliliter, counted by a lab technician as seen under a microscope); motility (the "wiggle factor"—the percentage of sperm moving consistently forward as opposed to sluggish, circular movement or no movement at all); and morphology (percentage of normally shaped sperm—those with oval-shaped heads and long tails as opposed to small, double, or no heads and no tails or twin tails).

The volume of semen is also noted along with the color, viscosity, pH level, and liquefaction time. It may also be tested for fructose and infections.

To deliver a semen specimen, a man is usually asked to refrain from intercourse for a few days. Then on the day of his appointment, he comes to the doctor's office or the lab, is provided with a private room, and is instructed to masturbate into a sterile container, making sure to collect all the seminal fluid.

The procedure is physically painless; all a man has to do is provide his semen. But that can be a problem. It's not uncommon for men to feel so tense and pressured to "perform" in an unfamiliar place—certainly not conducive to sexual arousal—that they simply cannot produce a specimen right then.

As embarrassing as most men find this, it's important to realize that nurses, doctors, and lab technicians understand. If it happens to you, just tell them you were unsuccessful; they'll usually ask you to try at home and bring the sample in as soon as possible (within about thirty minutes). Another way to ease the pressure is to let your wife help.

A special kind of nonspermicidal condom is available for men who are unable or unwilling to masturbate. Using this, they can collect the sample during intercourse.

If these methods are not acceptable, a sample can be collected by using coitus interruptus where, during intercourse, the husband pulls out of his wife's vagina in time to ejaculate into a container. The post-coital test may also give a clue to his sperm count. These last two methods, however, usually produce sperm samples that are not an accurate picture of the man's fertility.

Since so many factors influence sperm count, even from one day to the next, the man is often asked to give several semen samples over a period of several months. The whole thing may be an inconvenience, but the information it yields is essential.

Testicular biopsy. A testicular biopsy can give clues as to why a semen analysis shows few or no sperm. The doctor makes a tiny incision in the scrotum and takes a tissue sample from the testicle. The tissue is then observed under a microscope. If it is normal (showing that the testicles are producing sperm cells), chances are the problem is caused by a blockage or an infection somewhere along the way between the testicles and the penis where sperm are ejaculated.

This operation, often performed on an outpatient basis, usually requires local or general anesthesia. The pain is present, but not excruciating. According to Sherman Silber, it's more "like having a headache in the testicles for a few days."[2]

Vasogram. The vasogram is an X-ray of the blood flow through the tubes which carry the sperm from the testicles through the penis. It is usually performed while the man is under anesthesia and often in conjunction with the testicular biopsy. The surgeon inserts a small needle into the vas deferens and injects a radio opaque dye into the tubes. X-rays are then taken; interruption in the flow of the dye generally indicates a site of a blockage.

What Tests Can Tell

A thorough investigation might reveal one or more of the following problems.

Intercourse: Timing and Technique

There is no magic position or suave technique that will ensure a pregnancy. However, most doctors recommend that a woman not get up and douche or take a tub bath immediately after intercourse. A little "cuddle time" after making love will usually give the sperm sufficient time to make the journey through the vagina, the cervix, the uterus, and into the fallopian tubes.

Some couples, though, are not having intercourse at the time conception is most likely to occur. The sharp rise in a woman's basal body temperature does indicate that progesterone is being produced and ovulation has probably taken place; however, some couples wait until they see the rise, then have intercourse. By this time, the cervix may be closing and the cervical mucus thickening so the sperm can't swim through. The best time to have intercourse is just before the temperature rise. Of course, if your periods and ovulation are irregular, trying to outguess your body can be frustrating. But for a few people, something as simple as correct timing can lead to a pregnancy.

Some problems aren't quite so easy to treat.

Problems in the Female

Abnormal ovulation. Failure to ovulate (or irregular ovulation) is usually the result of some sort of hormone imbalance. If this is so, hormone replacement therapy may be administered.

Sometimes irregular ovulation is caused by an overactive pituitary gland producing too much prolactin (thus decreasing production of LH and FSH). Bromocriptine (Parlodel) is a drug used to treat this condition. Prednisone is sometimes given to reduce the amount of male hormone (testosterone) in the system. This may encourage ovulation.

Perhaps the most popular drug used to stimulate ovulation is clomiphene citrate (Clomid or Serophene). Generally used in women with fertile husbands and some estrogen production, this drug stimulates the pituitary gland to produce more LH and FSH. These hormones in turn stimulate the ovaries to produce and release eggs. The majority of proper candidates taking clomiphene do ovulate.

If clomiphene is not successful, sometimes the doctor will add an injection of HCG (human chorionic gonadotropin). This drug acts like LH to cause the release of eggs in many women.

If this therapy doesn't result in ovulation, the woman may need extra FSH also, which encourages the ovaries to produce mature eggs. In this case, HCG may be given in conjunction with HMG (human menopausal gonadotropin, or Pergonal). Pergonal injections are powerful, expensive, and potentially dangerous unless administered by a knowledgeable physician. If you're on Pergonal, your response to the drug will be monitored frequently by ultrasound and blood and urine tests to avoid hyperstimulation of the ovaries.

If these drugs do not cause ovulation, sometimes a wedge resection of the ovaries will help. Removing a wedge of tissue from the ovary produces ovulation in many women; however, this is usually a last resort, since scarring of the ovaries may result from the surgery itself.

Cervical factors. Structural abnormalities in the cervix may contribute to infertility. Cervical stenosis (where the cervix narrows, preventing sperm from passing through), polyps (which may block the entrance to the uterus), or a condition doctors call an "incompetent cervix" (where the cervix is not strong enough to sustain a pregnancy) may all prevent a full-term pregnancy. More often, though, problems with the cervix concern the mucus.

Cervical mucus that is "hostile" to sperm may be so for several reasons. Normally, during a woman's cycle, her mucus changes in response to estrogen. Just prior to ovulation, increased estrogen production results in mucus that is thin and stringy and easily penetrated by sperm. If not enough estrogen is produced, the mucus may remain too thick and block the passage of sperm to the uterus. Estrogen may be given during the first half of the cycle to stimulate production of thin mucus that will allow sperm to pass through.

Infections can also kill or immobilize sperm. These are usually treated with antibiotics.

Sometimes antibodies in the woman's cervix attack her husband's sperm as foreign substances in her body. It's not known why this reaction exists, but when a woman's antibodies have responded to her husband's sperm this way once, they are quick to attack sperm each successive time they enter her body. This condition may be treated with steroids or condom therapy—using a condom for several months during sexual intercourse until her antibody reaction decreases or disappears.

Scarred tubes. Scarring on the outside of the fallopian tubes (usually diagnosed during a laparoscopy) inhibits their movement; scarring on the inside (diagnosed by a hysterosalpingogram) blocks the passageway between the ovaries and the uterus. Both conditions inhibit the tubes' ability to pick up the egg and pass it along toward oncoming sperm.

Tubal scarring is often caused by some prior infection, ranging from one a woman never even knew she had to a painful case of pelvic inflammatory disease (PID). Endometriosis may also cause tubal scarring.

The condition might be treated by laser surgery; however, if a tube is completely obstructed, sometimes the blocked portion must be removed and the tube ends reconnected using microsurgery.

Endometriosis. Usually diagnosed by a laparoscopy, endometriosis occurs when pieces of endometrial tissue (the mucous membrane lining the uterus) are found attached to the abdominal wall and internal organs. These implants bleed whenever menstruation occurs, causing pain and scarring of the organs in the abdominal cavity.

Endometriosis can be very mild (some women don't know they have it until the doctor discovers it) and treatable with drug therapy or surgery during the laparoscopy. However, more severe cases may require major surgery.

Birth control pills taken daily are sometimes prescribed to stop menstruation and give the implants a chance to heal. Danazol (Danocrine), a synthetic male hormone, has also been used successfully to eliminate endometriosis by stopping FSH and LH production and producing a "false menopause." This, too, gives implants a chance to heal.

Surgery may also be used to treat endometriosis, although most physicians prefer to try the drug therapy first, since the surgery itself can produce more scarring.

Uterine abnormalities. Defects in the uterine structure are relatively rare, but one of the most common of these is a heart-shaped uterus with a septum (wall) which can divide the uterus in two. A hysterosalpingogram, hysteroscopy, and laparoscopy give more details about the severity of this structural problem. Depending on the severity, a surgeon can correct it either during a hysteroscopy or major surgery.

Fibroid tumors which can form within the uterus are usually benign but can keep an embryo from implanting or block the entrance to the fallopian tube. Major abdominal surgery is required to remove fibroids.

Uterine infections may also result in infertility. These are usually treated with antibiotics and a D & C (dilatation and curettage, where the cervix is dilated and the uterine lining scraped) if the antibiotics are unsuccessful. If the infection is severe enough to produce scarring within the uterus, this scar tissue can often be removed during a hysteroscopy.

Problems in the Male

Varicocele. A varicocele (varicose vein in the scrotum) is one of the most common contributors to infertility in men. A varicocele usually forms in the man's left testicle, when the valves that keep blood from pooling in the testicles break down, and the vein swells because of the increased blood pressure put on it. Exactly why this affects a man's sperm count is not known. However, the most widely accepted theory is that the blood collected in the veins creates too much heat for healthy sperm production and survival.

A varicocele can be diagnosed during a physical examination. Treatment involves surgery under local or general anesthesia, where an incision is made in the lower abdomen and the vein is tied off to prevent blood from pooling; the blood then finds alternate routes back up through the body.

Most men (about 70 percent) experience an improved sperm count by six to eight months after the operation.[3] About half of these actually impregnate their wives.

Ductal obstruction. If a semen analysis shows no sperm, yet a testicular biopsy reveals the presence of sperm cells in the testicle, most physicians suspect a blockage somewhere in the tubes that transport sperm. Infections can cause ductal obstruction; so can scar tissue from previous surgery. A few men are born with ductal abnormalities.

Some men can be helped by surgery, although raising a sperm count to normal fertile levels hasn't been terribly successful; however, surgical techniques are improving all the time.

Undescended testicles (cryptorchidism). Occasionally a man is born with his testicles still "hidden" in the abdomen, rather than descended into the scrotum. Since the temperature inside the body is too high for sperm production, he is most often infertile.

The testicles can be lowered either by hormone injections or by surgery. However, this condition must be treated at an early age (under five or six years old) in order for the testicles to retain their ability to manufacture sperm.

Testicular damage. Normally the mumps virus won't harm the testicles of boys, but it can destroy a man's fertility if he catches it in adulthood. If the illness is treated in time, doctors can prevent total damage to the testicles.

A blow to the testicles can also cause damage which may require surgery, and sometimes surgery itself in this area of the body can damage testicles accidentally.

Ejaculatory problems. The most common fertility-related ejaculatory problem in men is retrograde ejaculation, where semen is squirted back into the bladder rather than out through the penis. This condition may affect men who have had surgery on the nerves in the bladder area or men who have diabetes.

To help overcome this problem, semen can be re-trieved through a catheter and introduced into the man's wife through artificial insemination.

Hormonal problems. Hormonal problems are seldom the culprits in male infertility. If tests show the male deficient in a particular hormone, hormone replacement therapy offers hope. More often than not, male infertility is a mystery and hormones are given on a trial basis. Men have taken drugs such as Clomid, Pergonal, HCG, Cyto-mel (a thyroid derivative), cortisone, and HMG without much success.

Antibodies. A man may produce antibodies that at-tack his own sperm. These can be detected in blood serum or seminal fluid. Unfortunately, an effective treatment for these antibodies has not been developed.

Other factors. A number of other things can affect sperm count: viral and bacterial infections (even dental abscesses); radiation (those who work with X-rays are particularly at risk); chemicals (such as agent orange); diet (vitamins C and E and the mineral zinc have been given to infertile men); heat (often men are instructed to wear boxer shorts instead of briefs and to avoid hot baths); high altitudes; drugs (including alcohol and even large doses of aspirin); and genetic problems (such as Klinefelter's Syn-drome, a rare disease in which a man carries one or more extra X chromosomes in his cells).

So Help Me Get Through All This

Along with the diagnosis and treatment of infertility comes anxiety for many people. You may be one who can undergo surgery without a worry; you may not agonize about experiencing discomfort or bodily changes. In that case, you're a rare breed. Most of us find the entire investi-gation rather frightening. One of the best ways to get through it all is to confront those fears with facts. For instance, many men and women have some fear of doctors, drugs and their side effects, physical pain, surgery, and the duration of the investigation itself.

The Doctor

The letters M.D. are often intimidating, especially since as infertility patients we're feeling vulnerable and helpless anyway. Yes, the doctor went to medical school, but just because you didn't doesn't mean you should let the doctor do all of your thinking and choosing. On the other hand, cooperation with your physician is essential if you want help. For this reason, it's important that you choose a doctor you can trust. Look for one who:

1. *Invites your questions*. Write them down as you think of them before your appointment—and write down the doctor's answers, too. Don't come to the office without a notebook. Often people will compose entire lists in their heads, only to forget it all when they're nose to nose with a medical expert.

2. *Is honest* about what to expect from treatments and about the limits of his or her own knowledge. Your doctor should be willing to refer you elsewhere if necessary.

3. *Is compassionate and understanding* of the stresses of infertility. I have to smile when I think of the box of tissues my doctor keeps handy in his office. It's a sign to me that he knows tears are a part of infertility, and quite justified.

4. *Is knowledgeable and competent* in the area of infertility. You may be fond of your gynecologist, but your gynecologist may not be primarily concerned with infertility. A specialist can often save you precious time and money in the long run.

Furthermore, a physician whose expertise lies in infertility can spare you some emotional discomfort. I was apprehensive and fearful as I made our first appointment with a fertility specialist, yet the man's office actually became a comfort as I settled in the waiting room. I saw literature about RESOLVE and infertility—no *Baby Talk* magazines, no kids on mothers' laps, no cracker crumbs on the floor, no pregnant women. There were pictures of babies born to formerly infertile couples, pictures of fertilized eggs dividing for in vitro fertilization. And in the examining room, I lay back on the table, looked at the ceiling, and saw a picture of conception—an egg meeting sperm. The whole place was itself a picture of hope.

Drugs and Their Side Effects

If you're one who hates to take so much as an aspirin, taking drugs to correct infertility problems may make you uneasy. However, a little bit of information can go a long way in easing your mind. Before you take a drug, make sure you know:

1. *Exactly what it's supposed to correct and how.*

2. *The side effects of the drug.* Serono Laboratories Inc., manufacturers of Serophine (clomiphene citrate), publish some adverse reactions experienced by women who have used the drug. The list includes ovarian enlargement, abdominal bleeding, visual symptoms (blurring, seeing spots and flashes), nausea and vomiting, dizziness, depression, weight gain, and reversible hair loss. A pretty frightening list. Keep in mind, however, that all these symptoms occurred in a small minority of patients. (For

instance, weight gain was noted in 0.6 percent of women who used the drug.)

3. What will be done if you have an adverse reaction to the drug. Many drugs require diligent monitoring of your body's reaction; you'll be carefully watched. In addition, most physicians start treatment with the lowest possible effective dosage.

Physical Pain

Some tests and treatments are a bit uncomfortable. Some just plain hurt. Medically there are a few things doctors can do to ease pain: apply paracervical blocks, give sedatives, and administer anesthesia. But there will be times when none of these are appropriate, and you will have to hurt some. More than anything else, it has helped me to:

1. Remind myself that the pain is not permanent; it will go away.

2. Focus on the desired result rather than the painful test. Just about everything you want in life costs something. Haven't you worked toward a goal, suffered and sacrificed in the process, and pronounced it all worthwhile in the end? Even childbirth hurts.

3. Keep in mind that physical pain can force us to stretch and grow in ways we never imagined.

Surgery

Even if they don't verbalize their apprehension, most people don't look forward to surgery. It can provide vital information about your infertility; it is also the ultimate act of making yourself vulnerable. "What if I never come out of the anesthesia?" you might worry. Highly unlikely. You're at a bigger risk when you get in your car and drive to the hospital. "And what if they find something really wrong in there?" Then they can set to work making it really right. The agony of wondering is usually worse than knowing you're working to correct a specific problem. If you're having anxiety attacks about surgery, it will help you to:

1. Find out all about the procedure. Why is it being done? Exactly how will it be done? How successful is it likely to be? How long will it take to recuperate? Is there any way it can be avoided? And don't be afraid to express your fears to your doctor.

2. Talk to others who have had the same operation. The personal experience of someone else can be reassuring.

3. Tell your church family about your surgery. Allowing other people to minister to you at this time can strengthen you before, during, and afterward.

The Duration of the Investigation

Sometimes you may think "This will go on forever, won't it?" No, it won't. For a number of reasons, the investigation will end. It may end itself. For instance, you may have problems for which there are (as yet) no treatment. Or you may conceive and have a baby.

For many couples, though, the investigation goes on and on, and you as a couple must decide when to stop. Sometimes the stop is just a scheduled, temporary rest from treatment. At some time, though, you have been through every test, exhausted every option you consider feasible, and you are physically and emotionally worn out.

Your doctors may be pessimistic and still puzzled about your chances for conception. You are just plain tired of it all, and you long to enjoy life outside the doctor's waiting room. If you're beginning to feel like this, perhaps it might be time to move on.

Several years ago we went with some friends on a hike down the Whiteoak Canyon Trail in the Blue Ridge Mountains. Since we started on the ridge—the top—of the mountain, the first half of the journey was a romp. At 10:00 A.M. we took off, laughing and joking, expecting to be back at the car about noon for lunch. Downhill we fairly ran, past the three waterfalls, remarking about the beautiful scenery and wasn't it nice to be young and strong instead of old and wrinkled like the eighty-year-old man we met at the bottom of the canyon.

When we started back up the trail, however, we weren't so jovial. The mountain was steeper than we thought. Why in the world did we hike down so far? It was hot and we were sweating. No more running . . . we trudged. No more laughing and joking, only a lot of grunting. No more excitement, only hunger and thirst. We took our eyes off the gorgeous scenery and looked only at our feet. Would we never get to the end of this awful trail?

Finally, at 3:00 P.M. (having been passed by the eighty-year-old man at 2:00 P.M.), we stumbled into the parking lot, dragged our food and drink to a grassy spot, and ate (lying face down). How good it all tasted and what heaven it was to stretch out and let the earth take the burden of our heavy, aching bodies. And of course, the fatigue didn't last forever. It wasn't long before we could get up, nourished and rested, and move on to another activity.

52   *Part One: In the Beginning*

Jesus invites you to do the same. You may have started your investigation with enthusiasm and high hopes; maybe it's taken longer than you expected or been more stressful and painful than you expected. You may have been passed by others along the way, and that is so discouraging. Nevertheless, Jesus extends the invitation—as you tire, hunger, and hurt—to come to him for rest, nourishment, and new energy along the way.

> *"Come to Me, all who are weary and heavy-laden, and I will give you rest. Take My yoke upon you, and learn from Me, for I am gentle and humble in heart; and you shall find rest for your souls"* (Matthew 11:28-29).

Chapter 2, Notes

1. Marian J. and Roger W. Gray, *How To Take the Worry Out of Being Close: An Egg and Sperm Handbook* (1971), 18.

2. Sherman Silber, *How to Get Pregnant* (New York: Charles Scribner's Sons, 1980), 84.

3. Howard Frey and Jacob Rajfer, "The Surgical Management of Male Infertility," *Infertility: Diagnosis and Management*, ed. James Aiman (New York: Springer Verlag, 1984), 204.

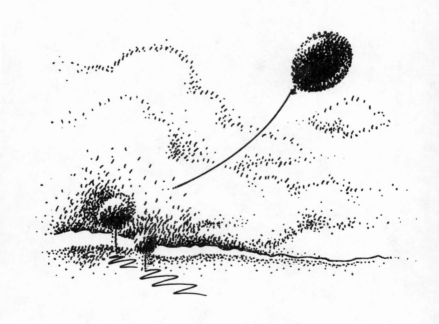

Part Two:
In The Middle

*This is Tuesday. Day 25 is Friday, and already I'm
holding my breath, waiting, looking for a sign, any sign of
pregnancy. There are times—like this morning—when I
want a baby so badly I can almost think myself into being
pregnant. What do I do with all these feelings? I've shoved
them around long enough. They never go away; they just
move somewhere else inside me and show up again every
twenty-eight days.*

Almost every woman remembers the day her period started;
it's the "rite of passage" into womanhood, an emotionally
loaded event. I used to read glorious accounts of girls who
joyfully anticipated this milestone. They celebrated its arrival
by throwing "I'm a woman now" parties and running to tell
their fathers as soon as they stepped in the door at night.

Personally, my experience wasn't quite so idyllic. I thought
I was dying. When I realized this was the part of growing up
the school showed movies about (while all the boys got to go
outside and play), I cried. I didn't want to grow up. If this was
the most wonderful part of womanhood, womanhood could
rot for all I cared. I loathed the discomfort and inconvenience
of it all. And every month I lived in fear of the sixth grade
boys snatching my purse, turning it upside down on my desk,
and exposing my secret.

Of course, as time passed my attitude mellowed a bit, and as
young teenagers, my friends and I referred to our monthly
menses as "Uncle Charlie." When Uncle Charlie (known in

other parts of the county as "Aunt Flo") came to visit, we tiptoed around his hostess for a few days in sympathy. Cramps made a girl mean as a bear. But Uncle Charlie's arrival gradually became accepted as a fact of life, and his punctuality was a sign of good health. At least I knew everything was normal.

In college I was much more comfortable with my womanhood and much less secretive about my body functions. A menstrual period was nothing my friends and I bragged about, but neither was it a secret we hid from our male friends. In response to "What's the matter?" all a girl had to do was groan "Cramps," and everyone understood. Then came the early years of marriage when Ben and I wanted plenty of time for just the two of us. We practiced birth control and actually welcomed the period every month (with a bottle of Midol) as a symbol of control. We didn't want a baby yet, and we were successful in delaying pregnancy.

But as infertility crept into our lives, we gradually lost that control, and the whole menstrual cycle became the focal point of our thinking. It seemed to push and tug our bodies as well as our mental health. At this point I began to resent it with more passion than I did when I was eleven. Every cramp was a fresh reminder of failure. And every month, new negative emotions erupted—emotions that festered and grew, mainly because I just didn't know how to deal constructively with them.

These were my psychological cramps—anger, frustration, guilt, low self-esteem, and most of all, self-pity. I could think of nothing else but myself and my misery, my obsessive desire for motherhood, my pain. I couldn't hear God, nor did I have much desire to, since he never answered my prayers the way I wanted. How I wish I had sought someone who could have helped me deal with my "cramps," the emotions which threatened to damage my marriage and eat up every ounce of my positive thinking.

The next few chapters provide some concrete suggestions on how to deal with these feelings, so often debilitating to us as infertile people. Some of the coping techniques may seem like superficial first aid, but I've learned that we live from moment to moment and day to day, rather than crisis to crisis. So these suggestions are meant to help you as an individual and as a couple through painful moments and trying days. Bit by bit they help you change your way of thinking, of talking to yourself, of relating to God. They will help you bring your emotions up to the surface where you can use them for growth instead of destruction.

All we can do now is wait. And how I hate waiting. I wait for test results, for my doctor to get back from vacation, for another month to pass so we can try again, and I wait for direction from God. I'm sick of this. How long can our lives revolve around my body's cycle? Around a stupid thermometer every stupid morning?

I got a letter from Cathy today. She's pregnant again. I want happiness for her, but when is my turn coming? I'm tired of trying so hard to be happy while I wait. Oh Lord, you know me so well. Do you cry with me every twenty-eight days? Do you hurt with me? I like to think so . . . but if you hurt for me so, why don't you give us a baby? Obviously we'll never do it on our own. You hold all the cards, and I feel so helpless, so weak.

3

Helplessness

If you are familiar with keeping a record of basal body temperatures (and if you're reading this book you probably are), you know that the thermometer begins as a simple, inanimate object used to predict ovulation and evolves into a third person in your bedroom. (We named ours Tom.) It's not so bad at first: waking up, lying in bed a few minutes longer to take your temperature (though you can't even go to the bathroom first). But after months—or years—you begin to resent the intrusion.

I had to kiss Tom before I kissed Ben in the morning. And after years of this, our sense of helplessness grew. In the beginning, it was a comfort to feel some sense of control: to think we could predict ovulation, have intercourse at the height of fertility, and get pregnant. Only I didn't get pregnant. We could predict my ovulation, we did have intercourse at the right time, but we were powerless to achieve pregnancy.

I finally got so fed up with Tom, I murdered him by "accidentally" throwing him on the floor. At least I had some power. Taking control had always made me feel better about my problems. In college, I had always been able to get a date (even if I had to ask for it). I could lose weight. I could make good grades. I could get a job. But now I couldn't have a baby, and my helplessness drove me crazy. I was used to getting what I wanted. And motherhood was something I thought was every woman's right. I was married, wasn't I? Ben and I had a nice home, we were established in our careers. We were Christians, for Pete's sake. The time was perfect but our bodies weren't.

We did everything we could to achieve pregnancy: the temperature charts, surgeries, post-coital tests, biopsies, the medication, the sperm counts, the mucus testing. You name it, we tried it. And nothing worked.

I was reluctant to follow an infertile friend's philosophy: "The Lord will take care of our problems. If he wants us to have a baby, we will, so I'm not going to the doctor." (I wonder if she would have gone to the doctor for a heart attack?) No, I just couldn't buy a "hands off" policy when it came to our infertility. However, after several years of treatment, we knew we had done everything possible. We trusted our doctors and cooperated with them. Still no baby. We knew we could either call the treatment to a halt or find different doctors and start all over again.

We decided to halt, admitting there was nothing more we could do. And there's much to be said about pursuing the investigation till you feel led to take the whole matter out of your hands and place it in God's. At least you know you've done all you can, and that peace can assuage your feelings of helplessness.

Here are some more ways to help yourself cope with waiting for the final verdict.

Make God as tangible as you can. Last summer we took our vacation at the beach. One morning I woke up at sunrise, quietly pulled on some shorts, and slipped out of the cottage to take a walk alone on the beach. For nearly an hour I talked to God about the things on my mind; of course, our infertility headed the list. As I looked out on the miles of ocean, those powerful waves and that fluorescent orange ball of a sun, I felt so small and weak in the vastness of such a creation. And he told me then, "See, Jill? I can control all this. Surely you can trust me with your problem." I picked up a shell, washed it off, and brought it home as a reminder of that morning and God's promise ("I'll take care of your problem") and his condition ("Just trust me.") That shell sits on my dresser today. It's a comfort when I'm sad and forget the time I so poignantly felt his arms around me.

A promise box is another way to help bring God down to earth. This is a small box filled with little cards on which are printed a promise from the Bible on one side and a prayer on the reverse side. You can find them in many Christian bookstores, or you can make your own easily enough. Keep it on your dresser, in the kitchen, even in the bathroom—wherever you spend quite a bit of time. You can pull out a verse any time during the day or night and remind yourself that God does keep his promises.

Most of us are tangible types. Any way that helps us touch God physically is bound to bring us closer to him and make us more willing to accept our own helplessness by acknowledging his loving power.

Read everything you can get your hands on. It's important for you to learn as much as you can about infertility. At first I thought my reading would send me deeper into depression ("Why fill your head with that stuff?" my friends would ask me). But informing myself made me feel less helpless and better able to ask my

doctors intelligent questions, to scrutinize procedures performed on us as a couple, and to make decisions about
which investigation routes to take. Ignorance is *not* bliss.
It breeds fear and frustration.

There are excellent books on infertility at the library.
Many will include personal experiences of infertile couples, understandable explanations of the male and female
reproductive systems, and descriptions of typical causes
and treatments of infertility. They are extremely helpful.
And even better, coupled with these books are good
Christian literature, not only concerning infertility but
also depression, anger, guilt, and self-esteem. Perhaps most
important are all the helpful resources for Bible study. At
the end of this book is a list of publications I've found
most helpful.

Act happy even if you're not. Somebody once told me
that the contestants of the Miss America pageant smile so
much, they put Vaseline on their teeth to keep them from
drying out. I wouldn't recommend going that far. Smiling
through tears may sound like a feeble way to treat a life
crisis, but it's really not. Dr. Frank Minirth in his book
Happiness Is a Choice advises, "understand your feelings,
but focus on your behavior. . . . We can change our
feelings with our will only to a certain degree, whereas our
behavior is under the complete and maximum control of
our will. How we feel does tend to affect what we do, but it
is also true that what we do can change the way we feel."[1]

Many times in the 8:00 A.M. classes I teach, I've
found that if I emulate my students (half or all asleep,
wishing for a pillow and a bed more than life itself), then I
feel tired too. But whether I feel like it or not, if I bounce
into the classroom (well, try), tell a couple of jokes and act
happy to be up at the crack of dawn, I actually feel much
livelier. This isn't to say that as an infertile person you

need to paste a Pollyanna smile on your face and pretend to the world and yourself that you aren't hurting. Rather, while you're doing all you can to cope with your infertility, you must dig down past the hurt, anger, and grief, and allow your faith in God's wisdom to spread up to your face.

I know it's particularly difficult at baby showers, births, and friends' happy announcements of a pregnancy. But try hard, even if it means smiling, congratulating, hugging, and then slipping away for a while. You don't have to throw a baby shower for every pregnant friend, but you'll be much happier with yourself if you practice genuine happiness for another person. Though you can't dictate the situation, at least you'll feel, with God's help, control over your response to it.

Develop a daily habit of prayer and Bible study. The feelings of helplessness have been among the hardest for me to deal with. Part of my problem has been my desire for complete control of my life. But of course, as a Christian, I know that if God is not in the heart of every decision I make, I am basing my choices on an unreliable source: myself. I've run after God too many times complaining, "I can't hear you. I can't feel the peace that's supposed to come with a relationship with you." The trouble is, those frustrating times generally coincide with a period when I've let my Bible study slack off and I haven't taken good time with God every day. Inevitably I find that when I get back into the habit of taking even fifteen or twenty minutes for devotion and prayer each day, I can hear him much more clearly, because I'm making a consistent effort to listen more intently.

Make the time, and put it at the top of your list—ahead of sleeping, eating, exercising, everything. Your spirit will be much more pliable, and it will be much easier to hand the controls over to the One who knows you and your needs better than you do.

A friend once told me that life is full of "in the meantimes," and if we can't live fully while we're waiting, we can't expect to live at all. We're so guilty of postponing life until we get what we want. We begin a diet and tell ourselves that we can't feel pretty or worthwhile or intelligent until we lose "X" number of pounds. In the same way, we feel that if only we knew whether or not we'd ever have a baby, we could get on with our lives—our hobbies, our gifts, our careers, and a right relationship with the Lord. The trouble is, those gifts could well be the very tools to help us cope with infertility.

The meantimes don't have to be so mean if we do what we can as humans, then lay our helplessness in the Lord's hands.

> And He has said to me, "My grace is sufficient for you, for power is perfected in weakness." Most gladly, therefore, I will rather boast about my weaknesses, that the power of Christ may dwell in me. Therefore I am well content with weaknesses, with persecutions, with difficulties, for Christ's sake; for when I am weak, then I am strong (2 Corinthians 12:9-10).

Chapter 3, Notes _____
1. Frank B. Minirth, *Happiness Is a Choice* (Grand Rapids: Baker Book House, 1978), 174-95.

Yesterday Ben came home from work and said, "Guess who's pregnant?" And before I thought about it, the first thing that slipped out of my mouth was "Oh no!"

I can't seem to be happy when the blessed event is happening to someone else. But I can't help it. I read in the paper yesterday about a couple with nine kids. They're dirt poor, and she's pregnant again. The injustice of it all is nauseating. Why is it that every Tom, Dick, and Harry can jackrabbit his way through as many and more kids than he wants while Ben—who deserves fatherhood more than any man I know—has to endure all this? Every month God dangles the proverbial carrot in front of our noses, then snatches it away. Deep down I know that I am blessed with much more than many people, and I can sit here and write about how God has some great plan for me. Yet I can't deny the heartache that creeps up on me as the signs of my period get clearer. I can smile, but I can't pretend to like the way God is dealing with my life.

4

Anger

I'm a door-slammer. Some people manage to release their anger in civilized ways, but my instinctive response to anger is to slam doors. I've broken hinges, jammed locks, and thoroughly irritated my husband with this behavior. (His response to anger is to clam up; I think it's healthier to slam doors.)

One day I agreed to take a neighbor to the doctor for her prenatal checkup. On the way home, she chatted about her plans for the baby's room, her Lamaze classes, and her son's excitement over the prospect of a new sibling. The knot in my stomach was the size of a baseball. When I got home, I walked in the house, slammed the first door I could find, and knocked the mirror right off the back of it.

We're an angry bunch, aren't we? It angers us to see expectant couples who can't afford or don't want their babies. We're angry when sixteen-year-old girls have intercourse one time and conceive a child they are not emotionally or physically able to support. We're angry when our friends get pregnant and groan about this one being unplanned. We can't stand it when new parents have the nerve to be disappointed because their baby was the "wrong" sex. Anger wells up inside us when people make thoughtless comments such as "Don't you think it's about time you two started a family? You're not getting any younger, you know."

It's even hard not to be angry when our friends who deserve babies get pregnant. Why them and not us? Many infertile people have a wonderful, generous spirit and are truly happy when their friends make the big announcement. One lady told me, "I'm happy for them, I really am. I'm just unhappy for us."

I wish I could say that my attitude has been the same over the years. Once I received a letter from a friend in another state. Since we're seldom in touch, I knew before I opened it that she was writing to tell me she was pregnant again. My first thought: "How nice." My second thought: "I hope she gets fat." Forgive me, Lord.

Don't we have a right to be angry? I suppose you could look at it that way. But be careful. Though anger is a valid emotion, it's important to deal with our anger in a constructive way. Allowed to smolder, anger will begin to dominate our relationships with others; it can destroy friendships (just because they have children and we don't); it separates us from God; it turns inward into depression.

So how do we deal with our anger creatively? First, think about the target of your anger. For me, deep down, it wasn't my social conditioning (which led me to view motherhood as my ultimate right) or my pregnant friends. I knew they could do nothing to make me pregnant. But God could. And he didn't. And that made me angry. I was continually shaking my fist at him, asking "Why us?" and losing all perspective and most of my knowledge of the wisdom of his timing. The angrier I got, the stronger my negativism became—and the further I drifted from him.

Eventually, however, I did find a few ways to focus on the positive. Try one or more of the following ideas if you find yourself angry and discouraged.

Keep a joybook. Every evening before I go to bed, I list—in a notebook designated especially for this purpose—all the pleasures of the previous twenty-four hours. Even the worst of days has its choice moments: a smile, a joke, an encouraging Bible verse; the touch of a friend's hand; extra cheese on your pizza; a walk in the fresh air. You'll be amazed at the healing power of filling a book with the rightness of life. This is not simply a "list your blessings when you feel blue" remedy. It's a continual feeding of your mind with positives.

So today you had another expensive test and you hurt and you just found out your best friend is pregnant for the third time. Your day has drowned you with downers. **Search out** the positives and write them down. Try it for a month, and see if it doesn't change your perspective—and soften your anger.

Turn your anger into something concrete (door slamming doesn't count) and give it to someone else. My second response to many of my problems is to look for the answer in the Toll House cookie. I'm the original Cookie Monster, and baking is therapeutic for me. The creative activity eases my tension; but the best part is giving them away. Most people are delighted to be remembered, and this takes my focus off myself. In the same way, you can bake bread (or anything else), cut grass, plant flowers—all for someone who needs it.

Anger does melt (at least soften) when you spend time

thoughtfully surprising other people with concrete expressions of your affection.

Try writing your anger out. You might enjoy keeping a journal in which you can be totally honest about your feelings. Setting mine down on a piece of paper somehow makes them easier to deal with. You'll find excerpts from my journal scattered throughout this book. They are not always positive or kind, because I used it as a sounding board for my feelings—all my feelings. But now I can look back through the entries and recognize the target of much of my anger (God) and take steps to come closer to him.

If you're interested in keeping a journal, you can begin with a simple notebook. (I started with an old spiral notebook, but now I like to buy hardbound wordless books with blank pages.) Your journal can be anything from a pocket notebook you carry all the time to a group of loose papers you keep in a box somewhere. Use it as your joybook, your sounding board. Be honest as you write, or the journal won't be a true reflection of your feelings. It won't help you cope or even discover what you're feeling if you write to impress some nameless somebody who may someday get hold of your book and publish it as a "true confessions" novel. If you need to vent your anger on paper and are terrified of someone else seeing it, write it out and then tear it up. At least you've released it.

Don't feel as though you have to write in it every day. You are not its slave; it is supposed to work for you. Just try writing on a regular basis, and through your journal God can help you learn more about yourself and your anger.

Pray "pretty prayers." This suggestion comes from Vicky Love in her book *Childless Is Not Less*. When you meet someone with children and find yourself resenting them on contact, pray God's best blessings for them. This can be tough—to pray sincerely—and it may take some practice. But it's a start. Rather than anger, it's a step in a supportive (and less self-centered) direction.

Direct your angry energy into some satisfying work. In her autobiography *Blackberry Winter*, Margaret Mead has said,

> Something very special sometimes happens to women when they know they will not have a child—or any more children. . . . Suddenly, their whole creativity is released—they paint or write as never before or they throw themselves into academic work with enthusiasm, when before they only had half a mind to spare for it.[1]

As we search for constructive ways to deal with anger, God helps us—if we let him. Replacing the anger with faith in him will "free our minds up" to do some valuable things. Had Ben and I never experienced the pain of infertility, writing a book about the subject wouldn't have crossed my mind. I probably wouldn't have attempted to write a book, period. But because of my experience and some valuable lessons I've learned, as well as the heartache I feel for others in the same crisis, God led me to try. It hasn't been easy, but I have found that in the doing God has liberated my thinking and allowed constructive work to fill the spaces that anger has left. And I believe I now teach my students more effectively because this work has made me so vulnerable and more sensitive to the pains and problems of others.

Try turning to your work, whatever it is, putting your heart into it and serving the people you work with. Turn to it—not to drown in it or hide under it—but as an effort to fill your angry spaces with growth.

Most of my teenage years were spent arguing with my mom about the length of my skirts. One day we were on the battlefield (a dressing room) when I fell in love with a little number that came about ten inches above my knees.

"Absolutely not!" she said.

"But why?" I wailed. "It looks fine!"

Her omniscient eye surveyed my form and she replied, "Not from behind." Once I broadened my perspective (in this case, the rear view), I saw what she meant. I couldn't even bend over to sneeze.

Isn't this typical of our behavior with God? With our tunnel vision we think we know what's good for us. We think we are broad-sighted and mature enough to know what's best and when. We get angry when the Lord doesn't see it our way. But he sees from up front, out back, and bent over—more directions than we possibly could. And it's in his perspective we must learn to trust.

> *Wait on the LORD: be of good courage, and he shall strengthen thine heart: wait, I say, on the LORD.*
>
> (Psalm 27:14, KJV)

Chapter 4, Notes _____

1. Margaret Mead, *Blackberry Winter: My Earlier Years* (New York: William Morrow and Co., 1972), 246-47.

I talked to the doctor today. The verdict is in. He said, "I have one more treatment to recommend."

"What's that?" I asked, daring to raise my hopes.

"Adoption. Ha, ha!"

Save the jokes, buster. This isn't funny. How insensitive could he get, anyway? After all Ben has been through, after all I have been through, together after all the drugs have been pumped into us, the needles injected, the knives sliced into our reproductive organs, after all the time we've spent in doctors' waiting rooms, waiting our turn to be poked and probed, grilled about our sex life, and charged exorbitant amounts for all the pain and no results—after all that, couldn't the man at least feel sorry for us?

5

Self-Pity

Not long ago, my husband brought home a box of 125 Reese's Peanut Butter Cups. "Wow," I thought. "With a little self-discipline, I could make these last a lifetime." But every time I passed the box, my one-more-won't-hurt mentality took over. (They were small.) In five days the whole thing was gone. I couldn't believe it. (Neither could Ben.)

Depression is like that. It starts as disappointment (one small one). No baby this month. Oh well, we'll just try again next month. Next month brings no baby, and the disappointment intensifies. Achieving a pregnancy becomes an obsession. With each disappointment you allow yourself a little more self-pity, and before you know it, you're wallowing in it. I know; I've done my share.

Tim LaHaye, in his book *How to Win Over Depression*, says the root of all depression is self-pity, and the only way to overcome self-pity is to face it as a sin. A sin? Ouch, that hurts. But I've come to realize that LaHaye is right; self-pity serves no worthwhile purpose.

Self-pity plagues couples struggling with infertility. It's easy for us to feel sorry for ourselves when our friends are having litters of kids; when we're forced to attend baby showers, our hopes dying while someone else's are being born. People aren't much help sometimes. Everyone runs into the lady who chirps, "We never had any trouble. All Fred had to do was hang his hat on the bedpost and I was pregnant." Good for Fred. All we can do is make him an offer on his hat (we've tried everything else). We have a right to feel sorry for ourselves, don't we?

My heart says "Yes, of course, you poor thing." But my head knows better. My intellect tells me that self-pity is in no way constructive—that it can only lead me to depression. LaHaye goes on to say, "When stripped of its false facades of excuse-making and self-justification, self-pity stands naked and exposed as a mental-attitude sin. Those who would be most hesitant to commit an overt act of sin such as adultery or fornication seem to have no compunction against this mental sin."[1]

Whenever you feel yourself slipping into a "poor me" routine, tell yourself to stop it. Then think about putting the following suggestions to work for you.

Be prepared for the time when you typically feel sad. As your period approaches and you feel yourself slowly focusing on every twinge, every ache, every sign of nausea or fatigue which could mean a pregnancy, try to fill your mind and body with other absorbing thoughts and activities. This is difficult, I know. But the more you keep your mind on other things, the softer the blow will be if you're not pregnant. Plan a special activity (a picnic, a short trip), begin a new exercise program (after you check with your doctor), become an expert on good health, nutrition, or anything else. You can begin at the library.

It has always helped me to throw some extra energy

into my teaching, to pray for my students, to make an effort to reserve some study time for the Bible each day. You could plan a party or just invite some friends over for dessert. With a little creative planning, you can greet the blues armed.

When you wake up in the morning, thank God for the good day it's going to be. Then determine to make it a good day.

Cultivate a friendship. Is there someone you've always wanted to know better, but felt that you never had the time to get acquainted? In college and high school, making close friends came naturally. We depended on each other, we sought one another out. But after I was married, my husband became my closest friend, and I found it difficult to juggle schedule and priorities. I had to work at becoming and staying good friends with others. Friendship fell into my lap when I was single; now it takes more effort.

Friendships can be cultivated, though. Edith Kilgo suggests a number of activities that may help you get started. You might make appointments with someone you'd like to know better, setting up a definite time and day to meet each month for lunch. You can take time to show you care by loaning your friend books, articles, or tapes about subjects in which she's interested. Try setting aside time for calling your friend each week to find out how she's doing; and when you know she has a problem, make it a point to get back in touch with her to see how she's weathering the crisis—or better yet, to see if you can help her in some specific way.[2]

A relationship that's nurtured can grow into a caring partnership, and you'll find it easier to avoid self-pity when your heart is reaching out to someone else.

Love recklessly. When I was in the third grade I fell in love with Donny Carver. He was a senior. I walked on air until one day I heard him refer to me as "that fat little kid in the red." That did it. I learned my lesson: unrequited love stinks. And thereafter, I too often hesitated before making myself so vulnerable.

However, Jesus never let fear of rejection keep him from expressing his love. So many people—even Peter—denied him and pushed his compassion aside, yet he kept right on loving without restraint. I believe he wants us to follow his example.

Part of the reason we want children is because they're so much fun to love. Children need attention, we say; so we feel free to kiss and hug them, to tweak their cheeks and chuck their chins. We long for children of our own on whom we can be so lavish and wasteful with our love. But why do our expressions of affection decrease as the object of our affection increases in age? Are we afraid we'll be rebuffed? Afraid we'll look dumb? Or afraid that someone will think we're on the make? As we grow up, our insecurities collect to the point where we're afraid to make ourselves as vulnerable as children do. And we miss out on a lot. Whether they appear to be or not, most people are hungry for affirmation, and I've found that giving that affirmation helps dissolve my own self-pity.

One way to lavish love is with words, both spoken and written. How many times have you thought to yourself, "She looks nice today," and never said it? Or come home to tell your spouse about a couple you thought was terrific, but they never knew you thought so. How about your minister . . . a special friend . . . even someone you're not particularly close to?

Not long ago I was thinking about a teacher I once had who had given me more confidence in myself than I ever dreamed possible. He believed in me more than I believed in myself, and this inspired me to write and teach like never before. I realized that, in a special way, he was responsible for the beginning of a very productive period of my life, and I had never even thanked him for it. So, even though I felt a little silly at first, I popped into his office and thanked him for the confidence he had given me—seven years before. These people may be surprised to hear from you, but delightfully so.

Writing has much the same effect, but with an added bonus: words are tangible expressions of affection that can be read over and over again. Here's part of a letter Ben wrote to me before we were married:

> Dear Jill,
>
> I love you so much. I would give anything I own to be with you now, my precious. I really don't know how much longer I can stand to be without you. You are the sweetest, most considerate person in the world. I feel you are a blessing; a gift to my life. You are the most wonderful thing that ever happened to me.

Okay, so it sounds pretty corny after twelve years. But those hearts and flowers sent my ego and my energy level flying—and they're still good for a nostalgic chuckle! Such written words can pull us out of the doldrums and set our minds on positive things. You might try writing letters of appreciation (not necessarily mush) to your spouse, a good friend, a teacher, your parents—anyone who needs to know they're special. Everyone benefits from a love letter—the sender most of all.

And what if words just don't seem to express what you want? Try making a conscious effort to touch more: your hand on someone else's, a pat on the back, an arm around someone's shoulder. Physical contact can sometimes say "I care about you" more eloquently than the words.

Become a hugger. Not long ago, *USA Today* reported that women tend to hug more than men, Southerners more than Northerners, and the people who need physical affection most—the elderly—hug and are hugged the least.[3] What a shame that we've come to a point where, perhaps in our preoccupation with our own problems, we've forgotten how therapeutic, how warm and healing a hug can be.

Oh, I can hear someone saying: "Sure, Jill. If I started a touching marathon at work, everybody would think I'd gone out of my mind." You don't have to report in Monday morning by bouncing into your boss's lap; neither should you force yourself to hug someone you don't want to touch. But think about the times you have stifled an urge to touch someone's hand in sympathy, or give an encouraging pat on the back, just because you were afraid it would look funny.

A few semesters ago, I put a note in my grade book—a little card with a heart and a cross on it to remind me to reaffirm my students by words spoken and written on their papers, and by touch. I was a little hesitant at first; I know some people are a bit uncomfortable with this kind of affection. And, human that I am, I didn't want them to think I was weird. But as I tried to nurture them that semester, they positively blossomed. People need "strokes" of one kind or another. Don't hesitate to give them freely.

Jesus touched often: the blind man whose eyes he made whole by physical contact (John 9:1-12), the woman who had hemorrhaged for twelve years and was healed when her hand brushed Jesus' clothes (Luke 8:43-48), the leper he cleansed with his touch (Matthew

8:1-4). Jesus wanted children near him, and I can imagine that he loved for them to sit in his lap, to be cuddled and loved. I'm sure he must have touched his disciples often, during triumphant times as well as moments when he tried so hard—sometimes unsuccessfully—to make them understand just who he was. And Jesus himself needed and loved human touch. Remember when he came to visit Mary and Martha? Mary sat with Jesus, pouring expensive perfume on his feet, wiping them with her hair. Of course, she was criticized for this "wasteful" display of affection, but Jesus was moved by it (John 12:1-8).

We should be so wasteful; for the surest way out of self-pity is the risk-taking, indiscriminate love that Jesus showed us how to give.

> *Therefore be imitators of God, as beloved children; and walk in love, just as Christ also loved you, and gave Himself up for us, an offering and a sacrifice to God as a fragrant aroma* (Ephesians 5:1-2).

Chapter 5, Notes

1. Tim LaHaye, *How to Win Over Depression* (Grand Rapids: Zondervan Publishing House, 1974), 104.

2. Edith Flowers Kilgo, "Making Time for Friends," *Today's Christian Woman*, January-February 1985, 65.

3. Lynn Howard, "Where the Huggers Are Across the U.S.A.," *USA Today*, 31 May 1985, 1.

I wish I could get this sadness out of my system and then let it go, go away. But it follows me everywhere.

Yesterday my predictable body told us no for the fifty-fourth time. I was so sad, even though I had tried not to get my hopes up. But I always hope, no matter what. Ben went to bed; I told him I'd be up in a minute. And as soon as he left the room, I fell apart. God seemed so far away, so cruel to create us with a desire for family, then withhold the family when the desire lingers on. I cried buckets. And I went upstairs. He was still awake, and I cried some more. I don't want to make Ben feel bad, but this time I couldn't seem to get myself together. So he held me, and comforted me and let me cry and heave and curse these awful cramps. There was nothing to talk about between us, nothing we hadn't already discussed before. There was nothing left to do but grieve—but at least we could do it together.

6

Grief

There is no funeral, no burial, no flowers or cards. And yet there is a death: the death of hopes for the wonder of a child emerging from an act of love between you. (Amid all the temperature charts and programmed sex, you'd almost forgotten that it is an act of love, that it's supposed to be fun and meaningful. You grieve for that loss, too.)

People express their grief in a variety of ways: tears, anger, work, food, drugs, alcohol, sex. Some don't express it at all. And grief is sneaky. Just when you think there are no more tears, no more anger, something will snap inside you, and here it comes again. In researching this book, I found in one library a large selection of books on infertility. But to get to the infertility shelf, I had to scan past the pregnancy shelf. One day my eyes rested on *Newborn Beauty, A Child Is Born, Childbirth Without Fear*—and by the time I got down to *They Say You Can't Have a Baby*, I was crying. I hadn't shed tears over this for a long time. Why was I crying now?

A lady in Barbara Eck Menning's book, *Infertility: A Guide for the Childless Couple*, expresses it well:

> My infertility resides in my heart as an old friend. I do
> not hear from it for weeks at a time, and then a moment,
> a thought, a baby announcement or some such thing,
> and I will feel a tug—maybe even feel sad or shed a few
> tears. And I think, "There's my old friend. It will always
> be a part of me."[1]

A part, yes. Not a bitter part, nor an angry one necessarily.
But a part that can make you in your grief more sensitive
to others' pain; a part that can redirect your energies.
Where can you start?

Let others share in your grief. I know it's nobody's
business why you aren't parents yet. I know that people
make insensitive remarks about why you aren't parents
yet. I know, in an attempt to make you parents, many
people take it upon themselves to dispense unsolicited
(and downright silly) advice that worked for Cousin
Emma who was pronounced sterile at age twenty and had
eight kids by the time she was thirty. Amazing. And all
she did was "forget about it and relax for a while."

I also know that your first unchristian impulse is to tell
them to shut up and mind their own business. But in order
for healing to take place, it's important to share your grief
(not necessarily every detail of the workup) and educate
people who care. Menning says,

> People should be made accountable for their remarks.
> This can only happen after disclosure of the infertility
> situation and what helps to the people who really matter
> to the couple. A person with a problem has the burden
> of telling others what the problem is and how it can be
> helped.[2]

Of course, you needn't feel obligated to explain your
troubles to relative strangers, but openness about the
whole subject may remind you that infertility is no sin, nor

anything to be ashamed of, even though it's very personal.

Ben and I don't hide our condition any more. When he had his first varicocelectomy, I had written "Ben in hospital" on my calendar, then erased it so no one would ask about it. He refused to be put on the prayer list at church, so only a couple of people knew, and it was a lonely time for us. However, when he went in several years later for a second operation, we asked for prayer and told people the truth when they asked why. And such support we received. People prayed for us, they came to visit, and best of all shared their own experiences, offering words of encouragement. We found that the same people who seemed insensitive in their ignorance of our troubles could well be the most helpful when allowed to share our hurt.

Join a support group for infertile couples. RESOLVE, a national organization started by Barbara Menning, has local chapters all over the country. They send out a bimonthly newsletter which offers readers' personal experiences with infertility and valuable information. You can also obtain literature through them on most any subject related to infertility, from endometriosis to coping with the holidays. RESOLVE makes referrals, gives lists and locations of local support groups, and offers the opportunity to be a contact person to another infertile person in the country.

Many people are hesitant at first to join a support group (you can join RESOLVE without joining a support group). Some find it hard to admit that they need help with a particular life crisis. But God gave us to each other, and the relief that comes from talking out your feelings with people who understand is worth the emotional risk and vulnerability you may feel at first.

Support groups can also help marital partners who find themselves grieving in very different ways. Though a couple mourns for the same loss, often their grief cannot be shared, and this isolation puts tremendous stress on their relationship. In a support group they may well encounter and learn to better understand people who respond to infertility in a variety of ways. What comfort there is in knowing you and your spouse are not the only ones who feel alone together.

Working through your grief alone is very difficult: you are reluctant to bore close friends with the woes of infertility, especially since no one can empathize with you like someone who's been there. Support groups can be a real godsend—a place to freely grieve, laugh, and draw strength from one another.

Pray for others. When I began freelance writing, I was tempted to let my discipline slide when the rejection slips came. One night I shared my concern with a friend who asked, "What are you working on now?" I told her about an article I'd started but had neglected for a while, and she promised to pray for me. Every couple of weeks she reminded me of her commitment. Just knowing she was concerned enough to petition God about my measly article gave me the impetus I needed to finish it. It was my very first sale—and from then on, I was a believer in intercessory prayer.

Previously I had thought of intercession as a frill in my prayer life. "Why pray for other people," I reasoned, "when God already knows what they need?" Well, I discovered one terrific reason: praying for others shifts my mind's focus from my own problems to someone else's, and in the process, my self-absorption slips away as concern for others moves in. Pat Jaracz has suggested several ways to follow through when you promise to pray for someone else:

1. Try writing down prayer requests in a special place. I use a note card in my Bible. As soon as I hear of a need, the name goes down on my card.

2. Focus on the spiritual, emotional and practical details of the need. For example, if you're praying for an infertile couple, pray that they'll be able to sense God's direction in their search for a baby, that their marriage will grow stronger, not weaker, as they deal with this crisis, and that their health insurance will pay a good part of their hospital bills.

3. Read Paul's New Testament letters for guidelines as to how to pray for others. For instance, he prayed that others would grow to understand Christ's love (Ephesians 3:18-19).

4. Tell people they are in your prayers. This reminds you to keep your promise as it makes you more aware of their needs. And everyone is heartened by knowing someone cares about them.

5. Finally, ask God if you can do anything else to help the person you're praying for. Then do it.[3]

When I made it a habit to pray for others, God answered my prayers for an end to my mourning, although not in the way I expected. I'm convinced now that an excellent way to heal your own grief is to comfort someone else in theirs.

Fall in love with learning. If you can't give birth to a baby now, try giving new life to something else: your mind. It may be that you've forgotten how stimulating it can be to fill your mind with new thoughts.

My favorite way to do this is to take a class, any kind of class. Is there something you've always wanted to learn but felt you didn't have time to invest—or just never got around to it? Swimming? Weight lifting? Flying? Dancing? Tennis? Or maybe it's time to give your intellect a kick. Ben has enjoyed courses in the Old and New Testaments. I took a journalism class that motivated me to hone my writing skills. That class changed the course of my career and filled me with excitement over the prospect of developing a gift I had neglected. Do you enjoy history? Music? Art? Poetry? Public speaking? Surely you have had dreams of doing other things besides parenting. Now is a good time to act on your potential.

In classes you meet fascinating people, stimulate your mind, sharpen old skills, and discover new ones. As Maya Angelou once said, "People aren't either/or; they're and, and, and." Try not to think of yourself as either a parent or a nobody. Concentrate on developing your "and, and, ands." Only then can you turn your grieving into growing.

Spend time acting like a child. Ah, my favorite. How long has it been since you laughed yourself sick? Or played till you dropped? Children have a way of giving 100 percent of themselves to pleasure and spontaneity, and we'd do well to follow their example more often.

Especially during the investigation phase of infertility, we become so obsessed with life on a twenty-eight-day cycle, we forget how to let go and frolic just for the fun of it. Our actions certainly mirror our thoughts, and a preoccupation with our sadness will translate into a joyless lifestyle if we're not careful.

One of my favorite releases is to put some good music on the stereo while I'm cleaning house and dance from room to room with my dust mop. We have an album of

Golden Oldies that's very effective in lifting my spirits. With this one I like to pretend I'm Mary Wells singing "My Guy" into the vacuum cleaner hose.

Or throw a party for no special reason. People love to be invited, and with a little research you can become a real connoisseur of games to serve as entertainment. Oh, I know; there will always be a couple of people who think playing games is just for kids—until they spend an evening at it. I have a list of about eighty games I've collected over the last fifteen years, and I keep a condensed list in my purse at all times (in case I'm at someone else's party and things get a little dull).

Of course, your choice of activities will depend on the type of people you're entertaining and the atmosphere of the gathering. But I've found games that keep people physically active are the most fun. Forget the chess tournament. Instead try playing "Hide and Seek" with a bunch of adults. Or organize a round of "Name that Tune" with golden oldies. (Don't forget to include Mary Wells singing "My Guy.") The Lord gave us all a sense of humor. Don't forget to use it in a spontaneous way.

One year Ben's birthday came in the middle of a depressing time for us. We had both been "worked up" and treated with no positive results. I wanted so much to give him reason to celebrate (or at least chuckle) on his birthday. After much thought, I hit on an idea.

With a friend's help, I brought a refrigerator box to work and wrapped it up in birthday paper. Then we loaded it up, brought it to his office where we were met by Mr. Flim Flam, the singing telegram man I had hired. I climbed into the box (which was on a dolly), my friend put the lid on and stuck a bow on top. Then the messenger wheeled the "birthday present" into Ben's office, sang

"Happy Birthday," and let him open his surprise. You can imagine his reaction when I jumped out at him—total humiliation. But we laughed that day more than we had in the two years before. In fact I'm laughing right now. And it feels so good. Laughter, spontaneity, play; they all heal in a special way.

> "But for you who fear My name the sun of righteousness will rise with healing in its wings; and you will go forth and skip about like calves from the stall" (Malachi 4:2).

Chapter 6, Notes

1. Barbara Eck Menning, *Infertility: A Guide for Childless Couples* (Englewood Cliffs, N. J.: Prentice-Hall, 1977), 116-17.

2. Ibid., 154.

3. Pat Jaracz, "How to Follow Through on 'I'll Pray for You,' " *Guideposts*, January 1984, 22-23.

I guess Carolyn really deserves to be a mother more than I do. She thoroughly cleans her house twice a year; she fixes Jim's breakfast every morning; she's always doing stuff like fixing Easter baskets for other people's kids, making candy, sewing pillows and clothes, canning vegetables—the perfect picture of domesticity. Compared to her I'm a home wrecker, not a homemaker. What kind of mother would I make, anyway?

7

Low Self-Esteem

A few years ago I had an appointment to get my picture taken for Ben's Christmas present. Of course I waited until the last day when pictures could be guaranteed for delivery by Christmas. And of course, I caught a terrible cold two days before. I couldn't cancel out at the last minute, but I felt miserable with my tomato nose. The photographer positioned me in front of the camera, dimmed the lights and said, "Okay now, give me a real sexy look." I couldn't help it. I burst out laughing and ruined the shot.

It's hard to think of yourself as attractive when you feel defective. That photographer hardly noticed my nose. No one can see your infertility. But your response to a physical problem can be a killer for your self-concept if you let it.

> generally each month no matter how hard i prepared myself for the worst, my hopes would rise. my heart quivering, waiting, grabbing on the thread of faith deep inside. the period would arrive. a feeling of defectiveness would take over my thinking. for years subconsciously i knew it was there. now it was surfacing in a way i could not control.[1]

Ann Kiemel Anderson's feelings are probably similar to your own. Many infertile couples suffer from feelings of worthlessness, or at least low self-esteem. And although they shouldn't, it's not hard to understand why they do. We grow up thinking anybody and everybody has babies. It's easy; God made us that way. You get married, then you have children. One seems as natural as the other. It takes no brains to get pregnant, no money, and no scruples—so it's not reserved for an elite group of people. Or at least that's what we thought. Now we find that although we have the "stuff" to get just about anything else we want, we can't seem to perform the most basic biological functions. It's as though we're geniuses at math and physics, but we can't learn to write our names.

With that mindset, it's no wonder our first question is usually "What's wrong with us?" Consequently, it's easy to see why we're so down on ourselves when we find out what that "wrong" is.

When Ben and I started our investigation, I was working in an office, with a new degree in English, trying desperately to find a full-time teaching job. After months of interviews, rejections, and a "you lose" from my body every twenty-eight days, I felt as though I couldn't do anything right. Ben had his moments too. He chided himself for "shooting blanks" or being a "bad rooster." Infertility worms its way into your self-image and eats away at it if you let it. It can have a negative effect on your marriage, your job performance, your energy level, and your relationship with other people. We found some of the following ways helpful in preserving self-esteem.

Keep an "upper" file. This can be anything from a box in the closet to a manila folder where you keep affirming notes people have written you, mementos, or your own notes of encouragement and praise people have given you.

I love to keep letters (the good ones!) from my students in my upper file. One came to me in the midst of our second series of fertility workups when I was feeling insecure about my sexuality and my teaching ability:

> Dear Jill,
>
> Not only are you the best English teacher I have ever had, you are the prettiest one too. . . .

I can hardly read it any more because the paper is wrinkled and worn—not from age, just from constant use.

An upper file is not a tool to build false confidence or to encourage you to be self-absorbed; however, it's so easy to forget—during a search to find out what's wrong with you—that you are very much loved, appreciated, admired, and gifted whether you have a baby or not. Keeping a file of positives and pulling it out to read when you feel down on yourself can remind you of your preciousness and worth. And if the upper file works for you, why not contribute to someone else's by writing them a note of appreciation?

"Change the way you talk to yourself," advises Frank Minirth in the book *Happiness Is a Choice*. How do you talk to yourself now? Do you curse your body every month when you fail to produce a baby? Do you expect too much of yourself?

I've always known that babies took up a tremendous amount of time. So a mother "had an excuse" for not doing much else aside from mothering. But I was a nonmother, so I went crazy trying to "make something of myself," trying to be the most perfect wife, at the perfect weight, trying to keep a spotless house while being the most dynamic teacher and the most brilliant pianist ever.

So much of my self-concept was wrapped up in my success in these areas that when I goofed (played wrong notes, kept the house in a mess, or couldn't answer a student's questions), I called myself a failure. At other times I was sure that my infertility was showing—that people could look at me and tell I wasn't 100 percent female (so I *felt*). Then I could talk myself right into depression if I tried. You may have done this yourself. But by the same token, we can talk to ourselves in a positive way.

Haven't you ever met someone who wasn't particularly handsome or beautiful, yet they exuded a pleasing charm and warmth? As you get to know the person better, you grow to love being around him or her. When I first met Ben, he had hair down to his shoulders, wore faded holey jeans and an old gray T-shirt. Obviously, I wasn't attracted to his physical appearance. Rather, I was drawn to his self-confidence (he was the biggest flirt I'd ever seen) and his self-discipline (he studied himself into straight As). Some people have such a positive attitude that they can forget their shortcomings and automatically draw people to themselves.

It's not uncommon, however, to find infertile people who respond to their insecurity in a different way: with a blatant display of their sexuality. In an effort to prove to themselves that they are still appealing and attractive, they may wear suggestive clothing or become flirtatious—even to the point of slipping into an extramarital affair. If you find yourself tempted in this direction, stop and think about what you have to lose: your marriage, your right relationship with God, and the self-esteem you were searching for in the first place. Engaging in indiscriminate sex is no way to affirm your personal worth.

On the other hand, you will quite naturally find members of the opposite sex attractive. Undoubtedly some will return the admiration, and when you're down on yourself, this attention may go to your heart, bypassing your head. What can you do when you feel the sparks fly? Don't berate yourself for your feelings; give them to God. Marjorie Holmes has done it beautifully:

> Don't let me feel guilty about this attraction either, Lord.
>
> Our time upon earth is short, and rapport between individuals, however briefly sensed, both sweet and rare. Don't let me decry it. Even as I forgo it, don't let me despoil its loveliness by being ashamed of it.
>
> Surely anything that makes us more acutely aware of another human being or arouses such feelings of joy and wonder isn't evil.
>
> It has made me feel newly alive, Lord . . . so I know you will forgive me when I confess that I feel this intense attraction. And understand when I thank you for it.[2]

So you're infertile—in reproductive organs, maybe. But certainly not in mind, heart, or even sex appeal. Talk to yourself a lot—and talk up, not down.

Set goals. When you feel inertia set in—when your ambition goes down the tubes with your hopes for parenthood and you're beating yourself because your need for accomplishment isn't being satisfied—set realistic, concrete goals for yourself. Write them down, work out a specific plan of action, and set your mind on reaching them. You may feel powerless to control your fertility, to achieve pregnancy, but goal-setting is certainly satisfying, constructive, and great for your self-esteem. You be the judge of what you want to accomplish. It could be anything from writing a book to cleaning your house to getting a degree to improving your prayer life.

Ron Klug, in his book *How to Keep a Spiritual Journal*, suggests that once you have clarified some of your major life purposes (such as having a good marriage, keeping physically fit and attractive) you can choose a category, an area of life (such as spiritual growth), and set several realistic goals for each of your life purposes. Once you've decided what you'd really like to do, plan your strategy and go to it, expecting to come out on top. You will.

Keep physically fit. This doesn't mean you have to pump iron several hours a day. But I know that when I exercise every day and make a conscious effort to eat balanced meals, I feel like taking the world and turning it upside down. And this exuberance transfers to my attitudes toward my problems and toward other people.

Research has consistently indicated that exercise is psychologically healing, although no one is sure why. Psychoanalysts claim it releases negative emotions that might otherwise be internalized. Learning theorists say exercise improves self-esteem: it gives a person a sense of accomplishment. Some also claim that exercise interrupts negative thought patterns. Whatever the reason, I know that exercise makes me feel good about myself. I walk for thirty minutes a day, and in those thirty minutes I can pray, give my mind a vacation, or work out my anger and frustration.

You may never have a perfect physique, but at least you'll know that you're making the most of your potential—and that should make you feel good about yourself. Many times you've probably felt as though you've lost control of your body: you can't get pregnant and there are times when you truly dislike your own system. Please don't. Fall in love with your body again—imperfect as it may be—and the things it can do for you and your attitude when you treat it well.

Maintain a balance of passions. One mistake many of us make is centering our lives around any one person, event, or position. When that one person lets us down, we're mad at them; when the event doesn't take place, we're frustrated and angry with God. I have struggled with this constantly in the past. I'd get attached to students and my attachment would turn into a dependence on their attention and approval. I'd decide to lose weight and I was impossible to live with until it was gone. I wanted a baby, and desire turned into an obsession. My life too often just wasn't quite right until I got what I wanted and what I thought I needed. And when I didn't? I'd ask myself, "Where did I go wrong? I guess I don't deserve it anyway, I can't do anything else right."

I've discovered that the best way to maintain self-esteem is to work hard at maintaining a balance of passions in your life so you don't depend too much on others. It's fine to be involved in church—if church is not your whole life. It's wonderful to care deeply about your work and colleagues—as long as your mental health doesn't depend on constant kudos from all directions. And the desire for a baby is a wonderful, natural thing—as long as it doesn't blind you to the joys of the moment and cripple your self-image; as long as it doesn't stunt your spiritual growth and keep you from reaching your potential in other areas of your life.

If you're knuckling under (depending too much on one person or event to make you happy with yourself), it's time to get back in touch with God. Dig deeper into your Bible study, pray in earnest, actively seek out his perfect perspective.

The closer you are to him, the more sensitive you are to his direction, the better you can hear him when he does speak to you. I'd be lying if I said I never needed other people to love and reciprocate that love, that I don't get high from compliments about my hair or my perfume, that I don't enjoy a laurel from my superiors at work, that I don't melt in the embraces of people important to me. But ultimately my self-esteem must come from God. He created me and knows my potential. And in the midst of balancing my other interests, he must be my ultimate passion. For in seeking him, I find the wonder, the love, the energy, and the joy that has been mine all along.

> *I will give thanks to Thee, for I am*
> *fearfully and wonderfully made;*
> *Wonderful are Thy works,*
> *And my soul knows it very well.*

(Psalm 139:14)

Chapter 7, Notes _____

1. Ann Kiemel Anderson, *Taste of Tears, Touch of God* (Nashville: Oliver-Nelson Books, 1984), 40.

2. Marjorie Holmes, *Who Am I, God?* (New York: Doubleday and Co., 1971), 160-61.

As I was sitting in the doctor's office today, my mind wandered back to one evening when we were first married. Ben's mother mentioned she had always wanted seven grandchildren. Of course at the time I joked that I'd do my part to help her out; then I filed her statement in my mind under "Someday when we have kids." Now it hurts just to think about it. We can't give her any grandchildren, and I'm so sorry. We can't help extend the family name, and I'm sorry about that too. In my mind, I feel like a little kid apologizing to my mother—except in reality I'm not quite sure what I've done wrong.

8

Guilt

I am a domestic disaster. I can't crochet, I've never canned the first vegetable, and houseplants wilt at the mention of my name. For a long time I wondered if I was fit for motherhood because I didn't fit the traditional wife and mother role—and I wondered if this was why God hadn't blessed us with a child.

For a while I felt that I had to turn myself into June Cleaver (Beaver's cookie-baking mom) so I could earn the right to be a mother. And I couldn't figure out why I was so miserable. The more preoccupied I became with every speck of dust and every dirty dish, the more energy I wasted worrying, "Am I good enough yet?" I compared myself with young mothers I knew, and decided I was guilty of not being the domestic type. So I tried to change.

It didn't work. No baby came as a result of my efforts, so I looked into other areas of my life for clues of unworthiness. When I heard someone say that God doesn't hear our prayers if we're holding on to some sin in our life, I flew into a panic, convinced that this must be the reason I couldn't get pregnant. Now a sin search can be a good thing, but not if you're trying to earn enough green stamps to buy yourself a baby—which is exactly what I was trying to do. I scrutinized every area of my life from my eating habits to my prayers. And of course I found plenty of shortcomings, plenty of sin. Thus I felt plenty of guilt.

Then I had to ask, "Why do I have to endure all this self-examination? Why must I achieve perfection before I can be a mother? Nobody else does." And with that thought came one answer to my guilt: nobody's really "good enough" to be an ideal parent. Children are a gift, not brownie points for good behavior. Likewise, the absence of children is not a punishment for past sin. If you are feeling guilty because of your past—abortion, venereal disease, drug abuse, adultery (or thoughts of it), or anything else, keep in mind 1 John 1:9: "If we confess our sins to him, he can be depended on to forgive us and cleanse us from every wrong" (TLB). When you ask for forgiveness, you're free in God's eyes, so start forgiving yourself.

Remember the man in the New Testament who was born blind? Popular thought in that day dictated that his blindness was punishment for some sin. The disciples asked Jesus, "Why was this man born blind? Was it a result of his own sins or those of his parents?"

"Neither," Jesus answered. "But to demonstrate the power of God" (John 9:2-3, TLB). And demonstrate he did. Jesus restored the man's sight, and the man told others exactly what Jesus had done for him. But until Jesus touched this man, he must have asked "Why me?" many times.

In a recent issue of *Stepping Stones* Leslie Snodgrass wrote, "My infertility was not an accident: it was allowed for some higher purpose in my life. But why? It's the 'why' behind a Christian couple's childlessness that brings such pain and confusion to their lives."[1] And indeed, we may never know why. But it's up to us to recognize guilt feelings for what they are—our own attempts to find a blame for our infertility—and get on with searching for what the "higher purpose" might be.

Here are some suggestions for helping you cope with the guilt you may feel along the way.

Approach Bible study from a different perspective. Verses such as these used to frustrate me to no end:

> Behold, children are a gift of the LORD;
> The fruit of the womb is a reward.
> Like arrows in the hand of a warrior,
> So are the children of one's youth.
> How blessed is the man whose quiver is full of them.
> (Psalm 127:3-5)

(Reward? I guess I haven't been good enough to deserve a reward as precious as a baby.)

> There are two things never satisfied, like a leech forever craving more: no three things! no, four!
>
> Hell
>
> The barren womb
>
> A barren desert
>
> Fire
> (Proverbs 30:15-16, TLB)

(How depressing. On the list of life's miseries, infertility runs neck-in-neck with hell.)

> If you can find a truly good wife, she is worth more than precious gems! . . . Her children stand and bless her; so does her husband. He praises her with these words: "There are many fine women in the world, but you are the best of them all!"
> (Proverbs 31:10, 28-29, TLB)

(Terrific. A noble wife has to have children to rise up and

call her blessed. I guess I'll always fall one short of ideal. What can I do to make myself more fit for motherhood?)

Everywhere I looked, it seemed, the authors of the Bible were extolling the virtues of motherhood, and I took it all personally—a dangerous mistake. Vicky Love advises:

> Those who walk in obedience to Christ are meant to receive His word with gladness. He has already stripped away our condemnation and He intends to eliminate false condemnation. What we must learn is to be heartened by the truth, not downcast because we cannot personally identify with every good testimony which someone else lives to God's glory.[2]

Just because our quivers aren't full does not mean that we have no gifts, that we cannot be full and happy. (There are many gifts, remember?)

And yes, we know how miserable and hellish a barren womb can be; the yearning for a baby can be like a "leech forever craving more." But we also know that the craving can be transformed into positive energy, and from that energy we can give birth to other precious and significant creations.

Proverbs 31 may be a description of a *good* woman, but we must be careful not to lock ourselves into a preoccupation with roles in this life. Jesus was certainly more concerned with the total person than with man-made roles of housekeeper and homemaker. In the same way, we cannot allow ourselves to become paralyzed with guilt because we don't fit an earthly definition of the Happy Homemaker. Dorothy Pape in her book *In Search of God's Ideal Woman* recommends that

> instead of blindly following custom or tradition, it seems
> best for woman to "choose that good part," like Mary,
> and sit at Christ's feet to hear his instructions for each
> situation as it arises; then attempt to follow them in the
> spirit He prizes so much. For many women these direc-
> tions may largely concern a husband and children . . .
> but God may also have some surprises for us. So each
> needs to receive her personalized operational procedures
> and Christ's power to perform them.[3]

The key here is to approach Bible study intellectually
as well as emotionally. This requires some extra effort on
our part. The use of commentaries, handbooks, and other
resources can give you a much broader base from which to
form your understanding of what the Scriptures say. And
you won't be so tempted, as I was, to fly off on your broom
when you read Scripture that appears to be a low blow to
the infertile.

**Realize that, yes, children are a gift from God, but
certainly not the only gift and not even the most important gift.** What other gifts has God given you? A nice
home? Open it up to all kinds of guests. A talent—sewing,
woodworking, teaching, athletics, hostessing, writing,
counseling? God can help you cultivate any talent and use
it in ways you never dreamed, if only you'll be open to his
suggestions. I don't know what your gifts are, but we all
have a responsibility to find our talents, ask God where we
should go with them, and jump in head first. Our infertility should be the catalyst for developing as whole people, rather than an excuse for beating ourselves with a
guilty stick.

Try making a list of your gifts, tangible and intangible,
on a notecard. Then put the card in your Bible and pray
each day for guidance as to which gifts God wants you to

cultivate and how he wants you to use them. Then . . . listen.

Don't rely too heavily on your feelings as fact. Infertility is a highly emotional issue, and it's important for us as its victims to try to be clinical and objective. Coming to conclusions based on emotions alone is dangerous. I can't count the number of times when I just knew I was pregnant. I felt fatigued, nauseated, and excited because I felt pregnant and was sure God was sending a baby our way. And countless were the disappointments when my period inevitably came. Month after month I set myself up for a letdown.

In the same way, if we trust our guilt feelings as fact, our lives will reflect a poor self-concept and a cockeyed relationship with God. Rather than trusting your emotions, trust God through prayer, Bible research, and studying the example Jesus set. He, of course, had feelings ("My Father! If it is possible, let this cup be taken away from me"), but his intimate knowledge of God had the upper hand in his life ("But I want your will, not mine" [Matthew 26:39, TLB]).

"Fact comes first," observed Quaker Hannah Whitall Smith. "The fact of Christ. Faith comes second. Faith in Christ. And feeling third." No matter how we feel about him, the fact of Christ always remains. The fact that he forgives our mistakes if we'll ask him; the fact that he created each of us with exceptional talents if only we'll seek to nurture them; the fact that he loves each one of us perfectly and has allowed our infertility for some reason; and the fact that only with faith in him can we channel our energies in the best direction, believing he knows what's best for us as individuals.

And feeling? It's important enough just to realize that as humans, we don't always feel the fact; but as Christians, it's nice to know that our worth is not determined by how we feel about ourselves at any given moment but rather by the God who created us in so many ways like himself.

Grow in the grace and knowledge of our Lord and Savior Jesus Christ (2 Peter 3:18).

Chapter 8, Notes

1. Leslie Snodgrass, *Stepping Stones*, vol. 22 (April 1985).

2. Vicky Love, *Childless Is Not Less* (Minneapolis: Bethany House Publishers, 1984), 123.

3. Dorothy R. Pape, *In Search of God's Ideal Woman* (Downers Grove, Ill.: InterVarsity Press, 1976), 361.

Last night was my "fertile" night, but I was determined not to let Ben know it. We were both dog tired, but I faked this big desire for a night of fireworks. As usual, he saw right through me and felt as though I wasn't being totally honest with him. Somehow we ended up in an argument, and who can make love in the middle of a fight? Another month down the tubes. This morning we both woke up feeling awful about each other. This is no fun.

I Can't Give You Anything But Love . . . Baby

When I was a teenager, I had some romantic notions about married life. What a shock to find out after the wedding that married couples don't normally loll in bed adoring each other. It took me less than a week to discover that sleeping together also entails a partner who hogs blankets, snores, and breathes dragon fire in the morning.

A few months later an unmarried friend of mine asked, "Doesn't your heart just pound when Ben walks in the door at night?" I hated to admit it, but I had to tell her no—sometimes it didn't even flutter. And this bothered me quite a bit. No one ever told me that married people fall in and out of love with each other so often.

I was afraid to admit my fickle emotions until I read Anne Morrow Lindbergh's *Gift from the Sea*. In it she says,

> When you love someone, you do not love them all the time, in exactly the same way, from moment to moment. It is an impossibility. It is even a lie to pretend to. And yet this is exactly what most of us demand. We have so little faith in the ebb and flow of life, of love, of relationships. We leap at the flow of the tide and resist in terror its ebb. We are afraid it will never return.[1]

Learning to love each other through routine ups and downs is tough enough; adding a crisis such as infertility can precipitate some more serious problems in a marriage. The financial strain, the agony of waiting for something that just won't arrive, the assaults on each partner's sense of self—all these contribute to the waning of joy and romance. As the wait wears on, there sometimes seems to be more ebb than flow, and in most couples, this is cause for more than a little distress.

The trouble is that for most of us, falling in love in the first place was pleasurable and effortless, so we entered into marriage thinking that a good relationship between two lovers is just "doing what comes naturally." Unfortunately, what comes naturally isn't always loving. A friend of mine tells of the time she, furious with her husband, responded to her basic instincts by throwing a dozen raw eggs at him—one at a time!

As Ben and I have hurt, we too have responded inappropriately. And when infertility came to us, we realized how quickly a crisis can separate even two people who love each other. Yet we found that with some effort (sometimes doing what comes unnaturally) the same crisis that split us in two could build a stronger marital relationship than we ever dreamed. Here's how.

THE PROBLEM:

There's no adventure, no romance in our marriage any more.

ONE SOLUTION:

Bring on the spontaneity!

There are three things which are too wonderful for me,
Four which I do not understand:
The way of an eagle in the sky,
The way of a serpent on a rock,
The way of a ship in the middle of the sea,

And the way of a man with a maid.

(Proverbs 30:18-19)

The writer of Proverbs assures us that the mystery between the sexes has existed for thousands of years. However, the rigors of infertility take their toll on the mystery quotient. And let's be realistic: you've been married awhile. Not only have you picked up his socks and folded his underwear, you now know his sperm count and motility. Not only have you seen her puffy-eyed from crying, you now know when she ovulates and when her period is due.

It's not hard to see how the romance leaks out of a marriage. But be assured that because God made us male and female, the seed of mystery will always be there somewhere. You've probably noticed that even with platonic and professional associations there's a special kind of energy that opposite-sex relationships generate. The differences between men and women can be frustrating, but generally, little quirks in the chemistry are refreshing . . . even productive. Thus it follows that in our marriages we can tap that energy source and bring back the spark that was there before infertility's demands smothered it. My favorite way: give in to impetuous, spontaneous behavior.

Be creative in surprising your spouse. Write notes on the bathroom mirror with a bar of soap. "Kidnap" her one day, but don't tell her where you're taking her. Look for ways to spring little (or big) surprises for no special reason.

Ask yourselves, "What are the most interesting, fun things we would like to do with each other?" Then brainstorm, listing all your ideas, no matter how silly they sound. Next, talk about the ones you both like, and try them. If you can't fit them into your schedule immediately, decide when you will.

A variation of this suggestion is the fun deck.[2] Here you brainstorm for ideas of simple, inexpensive activities you both enjoy. These can range from going to an auction to playing miniature golf to canoeing to visiting old friends. Then put each suggestion on an index card and pull one out whenever you like.

My favorite fun deck suggestion is going out late one night to get half a dozen doughnuts, each a different kind, bringing them home, sitting in the dark, and trying to figure out which is which by the taste. Another idea you might consider is following another couple around an amusement park all day, doing whatever they do. Use your imagination!

You can also bring other couples into the picture. One of our most memorable evenings was spent with two other couples when we brought all our favorite old records together. The whole night wasn't long enough to spend doing old dances and laughing at the music we used to (and sometimes still) love. If you decide to do this, you can reserve some time alone after everyone leaves for playing songs from your dating days and reminiscing.

Whatever you do, just make sure you do it as a couple. You're making great memories.

THE PROBLEM:
We're both low on self-esteem.

ONE SOLUTION:
Concentrate on nurturing behaviors.

One of the best definitions of marriage I've ever heard describes it as two people helping each other reach their highest potential. But when infertility barges into your partnership, two badly beaten self-images result—and it's hard to build your partner up when your own ego is hurting. Yet that's exactly what we must learn to do. Recognizing the problem isn't always easy. Most people don't come right out and complain of a bruised self-concept. But their feelings are often revealed in their phrasing. At our house, these lines often bounced off the walls:

"If you hadn't married me, you could probably have all the kids you wanted."

"You really wish you'd married someone more like your mother, don't you?"

"I guess I'm just not good enough."

Sometimes we're so absorbed in our own feelings that we fail to recognize the hunger pangs in a loved one's heart. We only see the behavior that the hunger initiates—the anger, self-pity, and depression. But it's important to look deeply into that heart: When he withdraws, what does he really need? When she complains, what does she really want? Now more than ever, you both need your worth affirmed often. You need to know you are cherished, and you need to be told in a thousand ways.

Try to praise your spouse at least once a day. I used to complain about Ben's method. I'd get a new outfit, come downstairs all decked out, and instead of "Wow, you look nice!" he would say, "Where did that come from?" Well, at least he noticed, but that wasn't exactly the reaction I was craving.

Gary Smalley speaks of a man who bought 365 pieces of wrapped candy, wrote a message on every wrapper and sealed them up again. This provided his wife with a year of good feelings as she opened one every day. If you're like me, you can feed on one juicy compliment for a month.

Imagine how your spouse would feel about getting a sincere piece of praise every day.

Take mutual responsibility for the burdens of infertility. Most counselors will agree that the more a husband participates in pregnancy and childbirth, the more closeness he and his wife will share when the baby comes. In the same way, the more a husband and wife share—physically and verbally—in the highs and lows of infertility, the stronger will be their bond. For instance, I have a friend whose husband stuck the thermometer in her mouth every morning and recorded her basal body temperature. A small task? Maybe. But in doing so, he showed support of her side of this pain-in-the-neck detail. It's nice if you can get off work to go to the doctor with your spouse, also. Anything you can do to share the load—though you may not be helping physically—will give your spouse a big boost toward feeling loved and sustained.

Try making a list of caring behaviors. Write down specific things your mate does that elicit good feelings from you, concentrating on ways your spouse shows love for you. (Aim for statements like "I love it when you reach for my hand in public," rather than "You're the best typist I know.") Share lists and make a commitment to express your affection often.

If possible, make emotional contact when you're apart. A phone call, a note in an unexpected place, a Gorillagram (a singing telegram featuring a reasonable facsimile of King Kong) are some ways of staying in touch. Flowers are usually a safe bet; however, they can have their drawbacks. When I sent Ben some for Valentine's Day, everyone in his office wanted to know who his admirer was, because, according to them, "Women don't send flowers to their husbands!" He in turn added all manner of bizarre activities to my "do list" when I wasn't looking.

Make spiritual contact by praying for each other. Linda Dillow in her book *Creative Counterpart* suggests acquainting yourself each morning with your mate's schedule and special concerns. Then, try listing the activities, concerns, and times on a card, making it a point to pray specifically about them that day.

Most important, make physical contact as often as you can. This week try to be aware of the many ways you can touch each other: hold hands in church, kiss for no special reason, find new ways to give love pats. Human touch is reassuring and—particularly in the midst of an infertility workup—it's important to remember that touching doesn't always have to lead to sex.

I remember so well one night when my cramps were giving me a bad time, the physical pain affecting my emotional state. So instead of using a heating pad, I pulled close to Ben, my stomach being soothed and relaxed by the warmth of his. I fell asleep, comforted not only physically but emotionally as well.

Say "I love you" over and over and over again. It never gets old. We can't underestimate the importance of these nurturing behaviors. They're fuel for the heart. And yet it's important to remember that though nurturing may (and often does) lead to true intimacy, it is not a replacement for intimacy. Lillian Rubin explains:

> Nurturance is caretaking. Intimacy is some kind of reciprocal expression of feeling and thought, not out of fear or dependent need, but out of a wish to know one another's inner life and be able to share one's own.[3]

In order for infertility's challenges to draw us together rather than destroy our potential for growth, we must stretch even further than caretaking into a willingness to share our deepest selves with each other.

PROBLEM:

We're not really intimate any more.

ONE SOLUTION:

Get in touch.

I hate stereotypes. Few things make me angrier than to be classed as a "woman driver" or an "emotional female." And yet, the more I study infertility and couples' responses to it, the more I've come to agree with Gary Smalley when he says that a major difference between men and women is "the tendency of men to 'externalize' whereas women 'internalize.' " Smalley goes on to say that "Men deal, in general, with the exterior world—business, industry, earning a living, facts, figures, politics, general concepts. Women are quite capable of functioning adequately in any of these areas, but by nature and preference they have a much stronger tendency to 'internalize'—to get into things at a feeling level."[4]

This can lead to communication barriers as a husband and wife try to understand their mismatched responses to infertility. I have found that women generally are much more open and verbal about their infertility than men. Women usually take the initiative to join support groups and, at first anyway, do most of the talking. They seem less reluctant to share their feelings with other couples. Between husband and wife, the typical pattern is something like this: she emotes; he clams up. She wants to talk about it; he feels "talked out." She wants to know his deep feelings at a given moment; he's expressed all the feelings he cares to reveal, and now it's time to analyze the problem and live with the solution.

Differences between Ben and me were the most pronounced about the time my period arrived. I'd shed tears, get depressed, and see no reaction from him. Then I'd press him: "What are you feeling?" "I'm okay." "Well, aren't you sad?" "I'm okay." "Don't you want a baby as much as I do?" "Of course." "Then why aren't you as upset as I am?" "Who says I'm not upset?" "You don't act upset." "Sure, I'm disappointed, but I'm learning to be content with what I have." This "solid as a rock" attitude unhinged me.

Actually, at the root of his philosophy was a strong faith; but like many men, he had also responded to the pressures of our society that tell men that big boys don't cry, that problems are to tackle, not weep over. A woman, on the other hand, is told by our society that it is healthy for her to express her emotions first, then solve the problem.

Our differing responses to infertility can be further understood when we consider that our culture encourages a man to find his primary identity in his career, a woman in her ability to mother children. To illustrate, my friend and her husband recently moved into a new neighborhood. As the women introduced themselves to her, she could see the big question coming: "Hi! I'm Jane and I have two kids." "Hi! I'm Joan and I have three kids." "Jean lives right behind you, and she has five kids. How many kids do you have?" Several other neighbors introduced themselves to her husband. They all wanted to know where he worked; no one asked if he had children. This helps explain why women more often than men seem preoccupied with having babies—societal pressures follow them everywhere.

A woman's "emotional" response is also provoked by physical pain. Vicky Love points out that "if a woman lives with severe menstrual discomfort two days a month, or twenty-four days a year, that means she will spend over two years during her lifetime in pain. This suffering will definitely affect you as a couple."[5]

All this is not to say that infertility hurts men less than women. Men are deeply affected, even devastated, by their inability to father children. A man's pain is just as acute as his wife's. But because of their physiological makeup and cultural conditioning, men and women often respond to the crisis in opposite ways. And this can obstruct intimacy.

Yet it's important for us to delight in our fundamental differences; if we fail to take pleasure in the novelty of the opposite sex, we miss out on the richness, the spice, the good old gusto that God wants for our marriages. How can we understand and blend our differences to create a true touching of souls? Our first step is to learn to communicate well. Here are just a few suggestions for getting and staying in touch.

Avoid the communication rut. Merle Bombardieri describes the communication rut that infertile couples typically fall into:

> She's miserable about not having a baby and keeps on talking about it in hopes that he'll finally understand why she's so upset. She also tries to find the magic words which will make him more supportive, because even though he tries hard, he somehow never seems supportive enough. He's miserable because he can't stand listening to her night after night, powerless to take away her pain. After a while, he only half listens in order to dull his frustration. She escalates in intensity to try to rouse him out of his protective fog. After she turns the volume up, he tunes her out even more.[6]

Sound familiar? Her suggestion is the "Twenty Minute Rule." Together set a limit on your "fertility talk" on a given evening (anywhere from ten to thirty minutes). Set a timer if you like; then agree to stop when the timer goes off. When this method is used, the wife usually sends a clearer, condensed message about what she really wants from him; the husband in turn becomes a more attentive listener because he doesn't have to listen for hours.

Be honest and clear about your desires. Try not to send "coded messages," communication which must be decoded to be understood. In other words, if you're upset and want to be held, don't get angry and freeze up when your spouse misinterprets (or doesn't notice) your need. Verbalize it!

Try a listening exercise to increase your ability to understand what your partner is really saying. Many marriage counselors use a 3-step cycle: (1) I send a message to you, (2) you repeat what you heard me say, and (3) I either confirm your perception or let you know you "heard" me wrong. This is particularly helpful when you're trying to understand what feelings precipitate your spouse's actions. For instance, once Ben suggested we call a couple and invite them over one evening. I responded with zero enthusiasm.

"Why don't you want to?" he asked.
"I just don't feel like it, that's all," I replied. (1)

"You mean you're sick? Tired?" (2)
"No, I'm not sick or tired." (3)

"Well, why don't you want me to call them then?"
"They complain about their children all the time." (1)

"Oh, and it's hard for you to listen to people complain about their kids when you want one so badly?" (2)

"You got it." (3)

Listen empathetically. When your spouse makes a comment or expresses frustration or anger ("Do you know how degrading it was for me to be told to go into the bathroom at the doctor's office and come out with a semen sample? I felt like all the nurses were in the hall giggling about what I was doing in there!"), respond with empathy ("It must have been really embarrassing for you"), not chiding or analysis ("Well, you'd better get used to it. How else can they get the information they need? At least it's not as painful as my workup").

Pray together. Few activities put me in closer touch with my husband than praying with him on a regular basis. You might want to establish a regular time for prayer together, praying especially for your mutual concerns, such as specific aspects of your marriage. You'll find that when you communicate regularly on a spiritual level, your connectedness will carry over into the rest of your life together.

Provide a loving, noncritical environment for each other. Most people will open up and share truthfully when they feel totally accepted.

I have lots of wonderful memories of time spent with my own father, but the best way to characterize my childhood relationship with him is to say I felt completely loved. Whether my actions were rational or not, I knew he would love me. I was prone to cry for no reason; he responded by kneeling down, offering his arms, and telling me I didn't need a reason. I was a chubby little girl with a big mouth, but he made me feel like a princess.

This love was most healing—to my insecurities, my hurt feelings, my despair. And what is our longing for a child but the desire to experience this kind of unmerited affection? And why must we wait for children to cultivate it? Why not learn to love our spouses in the same unconditional way?

How? In one way or another, ask your mate every day, "What can I do for *you*? How can I increase *your* happiness?" Granted, this isn't easy. Most of our marital conflicts are a continual—and impatient—staredown between partners as each waits for the other to meet their needs.

What a lonely feeling it is when we are both so emotionally needy we can't think of giving to our spouse; yet if we concentrate on each other's longings, our own will be met—the longing to be heard and understood.

PROBLEM:

Sex is no fun any more.

ONE SOLUTION:

Reread the solutions to the first
three "problems" in this chapter!

"Sex is the dimension of intimacy which is the most fun-filled," I read one day.[7] *Oh yeah?* I thought. *For whom?* The *Washington Post* recently reported that, according to sex therapists, sexual difficulties "are five times greater in couples with fertility problems."[8] In some couples, the sexual problem is the cause of infertility, but more often, the fertility treatment results in a temporary sexual impasse. And it's no wonder. Making love for us became a task with a goal attached to it, a sort of "Mission: Impossible." Actually you could hardly call it making love. It was making baby—or trying anyway. To be honest, there were times when I was so tired of being physically examined, I didn't want anyone to touch me, not even my husband. And there were times when Ben had given so many command performances, he felt our sex life was more like a circus.

Scheduled connections are something that infertile couples just have to live with for a while. There's no denying that you must have intercourse when the female ovulates for her to get pregnant. But we've found that our sex life is much more satisfying when we concentrate on enriching areas of our marriage unrelated to sex. The three solutions I've already mentioned are some of the best foreplay there is.

Be spontaneous and creative. Last Christmas, in an attempt to give Ben a romantic present, I made dinner and hotel reservations at the most elegant place in the city. I even booked the honeymoon suite. But for a couple hours after I hung up the phone, somehow the arrangements didn't set right with me. At last I figured out why: a planned evening centered around a bedroom was not what we needed at that time. So I canceled those reservations and made others for a weekend in the mountains. We love to hike and swim, and for one weekend in July, the physical activity and peaceful surroundings allowed us to release tension and gain a better perspective on our problems.

Think of unusual ways to surprise your mate—but always with your needs as a couple in mind.

Build each other up. The nurturing behaviors I've mentioned before are extremely important, especially nonsexual touching. Remember the kind of physical contact that used to thrill you out of your mind when you were fourteen or fifteen? Sit close enough to brush shoulders and knees; hold hands, touch cheeks, stroke hair, give back rubs.

Eye contact is also stimulating. Once, in college, I heard a speaker explain how, from across the room, his wife could make love to him with her eyes. I nearly fell out of my chair at such a romantic notion—but it certainly can be done. And don't forget the power of a wink.

Communicate. Try to understand that sex often means something different for men and women. Usually, a woman needs to feel loved and treasured before she wants sex. If she and her husband haven't exchanged ten civil words all day and he approaches her at night, she may complain of feeling used or devalued. On the other hand, a man often needs sex to feel loved. For him, sexual intercourse in itself is a comforting expression of affection and tenderness.

These basic differences certainly seem to cause a lot of problems. Just keep in mind that your husband is not an animal when he feels like making love after you've been arguing all day; your wife is not frigid when she doesn't respond. Among the other communication builders I've mentioned, try to concentrate on meeting and understanding your partner's needs. Also, reading and discussing good literature on the subject is a great help. I've listed some at the end of this book.

I once read that there are two kinds of people: those who are interested in sex, and liars. Though you may feel that your sexual interest is dying a slow and painful death at the hand of infertility, take comfort in the fact that the desire can be revived. It just takes some patient resourcefulness to turn a predictable physical union back into a love affair.

PROBLEM:

Our marriage is becoming too self-centered.

ONE SOLUTION:

Reach out.

If you've ever found yourselves as a couple withdrawing from friends and activities, focusing exclusively on your concerns, you're not alone. This is a normal response of a couple who's had it up to their necks with infertility.

A couple I know recently bought a summer home. "Don't ask my why," she said. "We can't even fill up the one we use in the winter. I guess we bought it just for something to do. But to tell the truth, I'm still so restless. I guess what we really need to do is get our minds off ourselves."

Projects and special trips just for the two of you are fine, but try to balance these with activities that reach beyond your own troubles. As the Clinebells note,

> A family can fulfill its potential only by transcending itself. One couple discovered that some of their most precious moments occurred when they were investing themselves together in a cause bigger than their own mutual satisfaction and happiness.[9]

Help people who really need you: the elderly. Buying and fixing up your own home can be satisfying, but you might also look for ways to repair or clean the home of an older person. Get the shut-in list from your church and adopt a senior citizen to visit regularly. Bake for them, talk to them. The elderly usually devour companionship from younger folks. They make wonderful friends, and they have a broader view of life than we have. (And they aren't continually getting pregnant!)

Try to be a permeable couple. Open your home wide—to teenagers, for instance. They're always looking for a haven where they know they can relax, have a good time, and talk to understanding adults who aren't their parents.

You might also look into becoming foster parents. Children whose parents are temporarily unable to care for them desperately need a loving, stable environment. You may be able to provide this and find great satisfaction in doing so.

Join an infertility support group. If no such group exists in your area, be on the lookout for infertility seminars offered by hospitals and other organizations. Here you'll meet other couples who share your hurts. Offer to help them through the crisis.

Teach a class together. Banging intellects can be a lot of fun for both you and your students. Ben and I teach a Sunday school class—a great starting point for intellectual and spiritual togetherness. And our sharing also benefits the couples in our class.

Break the "taboo" that we just don't bring our marital problems up front for the world to see. We talk freely about problems with crabgrass, our cars, even our jobs. But rare are the husband and wife who can share marital concerns with another couple. This is a shame, because we have much to gain from each other.

A good place to learn this kind of sharing is at a marriage enrichment retreat where the taboo can be legitimately relaxed. As most leaders will tell you, signing up for a marriage enrichment retreat is not an admission that your marriage is in trouble; rather it's an attempt to make a good marriage better. There are several models of retreats with varying degrees of depth and interaction between couples. More information on these is available in David Mace's book *Close Companions*. You can write to the addresses listed at the end of the book or see if your own church sponsors such programs.

Ben and I have participated in several retreats and will testify to the wonderful dimension other people add to our understanding of each other. And after retreats, many couples go on to be trained leaders themselves. This gives them a chance to help other husbands and wives learn how to take on the challenges of married life and emerge as real winners.

As I was reading an old textbook on marriage and family living the other day, I stopped at a chapter where the authors refer to the childless couple as having a "sterile marriage." At the very least, this is a tragic choice of words. Certainly there are moments when our bodies, even our marriages, feel sterile. The love that brought us together is there somewhere, but we are too tired—of tests, of waiting, even of each other sometimes—to seek it out. But find it we must and feed it too, for love is creative, and with its rejuvenation comes new life.

New life—in the form of a baby? Maybe, some day. But right now we can become creators of new life between wife and husband. As we take steps to grow together spiritually, emotionally, intellectually, and physically, there is no limit to the pleasure and fullness that can be ours—with or without children.

> And God created man in His own image, in the image of God He created him; male and female He created them. . . . And God saw all that He had made, and behold, it was very good (Genesis 1:27, 31).

Chapter 9, Notes ────────────────────────────

1. Anne Morrow Lindbergh, *Gift from the Sea* (New York: Random House, 1975), 106.

2. John Gottman et al., *A Couple's Guide to Communication* (Champaign, Ill.: Research Press, 1976), 201-15.

3. Lillian Rubin, *Intimate Strangers* (New York: Harper and Row, 1983), 90.

4. Gary Smalley, *For Better or For Best* (Grand Rapids: Zondervan Publishing House, 1979), 32-33.

5. Vicky Love, *Childless Is Not Less* (Minneapolis: Bethany House Publishers, 1984), 88.

6. Merle Bombardieri, "The Twenty-Minute Rule, First Aid for Couples in Distress," *Resolve Newsletter*, December 1983, 5.

7. Howard J. Clinebell and Charlotte H. Clinebell, *The Intimate Marriage* (New York: Harper and Row, 1970), 134.

8. Sally Squires, "Sex Therapy—Helping Couples Achieve Intimacy," *Washington Post*, 30 July 1986, 13.

9. Clinebell, *Intimate Marriage*, 205.

Part Three:
Is There An End?

I always thought I knew, but I don't any more. Where do babies come from, anyway?

The sex education books I read as a youngster used to baffle me. Most of them would begin with discussions about bees pollinating flowers and baby animals living on the farm. They would then tell me that a man and woman fall in love and get married, and eventually a baby would begin growing inside the woman. From there the authors would chronicle the growth and birth of the child. I found all this interesting but unsatisfying. I was too embarrassed to ask about it, but I just knew they left out a crucial step somewhere. How did that baby get in there in the first place?

When I finally learned about sexual intercourse, I thought I at least knew the essentials of reproduction. Then came a time when Ben and I not only had to learn about but also choose among several methods of reproduction—none of which involved sexual intercourse. Perhaps the authors I read during my childhood were not as backward as I thought.

You, too, will probably have to decide which forms of conception are physically and morally acceptable to you. This section can give you tools for making these and other decisions that come with infertility's territory—smart decisions that are best made with a clear head and a heart that speaks and listens to God in persistent prayer.

I guess what I fear most goes even deeper than my inability to have a baby. I'm just so afraid that I'll make the wrong decision and end up with nothing to show for it; that I'll walk around the rest of my life with a hole in my heart that will never fill, a sore spot that will never heal; that I'll carry with me always the aching sadness of a dead dream. . . .

10

Decisions, Decisions

Decisions were seldom a problem for me. Even as a young girl I had a systematic method for making rational choices. It worked well, and I still use it every now and then. Twenty-five years later, I even call it by the same name: eenie, meenie, miney, moe.

Unfortunately, this one scored a zero in making decisions about our infertility. The choices we had to make left Ben and me frustrated and exhausted. When we would finally reach the point where there was nothing left to try (and I derived an odd kind of comfort from that), I'd hear about another technique, another chance.

Yes, it gave us hope; but along with that hope would come more anxiety, more questions, more tests, more bills. And many times we asked ourselves, "How much more of our lives can we invest in a baby chase?"

Infertility, with all its mind-crowding options, can throw you into a state of mental inertia—a dangerous condition if it extends from temporary to long-term. According to Merle Bombardieri, the worst thing a couple can do is float into a "non-decision," where they evolve into childfree living, not by choosing it, but by letting it choose them; or by making a non-decision to agonize, setting no goals.[1] True, you may get pregnant unexpectedly; a chance for adoption may fall into your lap. But most of us at some point need to make some solid decisions—and the Lord has given us the brain power and resources to do just that.

Establishing a set of guidelines in making your choices—from changing doctors to choosing adoption—can be a big comfort as well as a real help in getting to know yourself and what you really want. The following guidelines are just that—suggestions, not granite commandments. To make the best use of them, add your own reactions to mine, write in the margins, supply additional suggestions. In other words, make the guidelines work for you as you choose parenthood or childfree living.

Step One: Establish Your Priorities

This will take some serious self-examination. Patricia Johnston, author and adoption advocate, points out some losses that occur when infertility steps in.[2] Take a close look at these, and ask yourself which represents the greatest loss to you:

Genetic continuity. Are you most upset that your family's blood line won't be continued through you? That you may not have a child who resembles either you or your spouse?

A jointly conceived child. You love your spouse, and have probably thrilled at the idea of making that love tangible by creating a baby together.

The pregnancy/birth experience. The desire for the physical experience of carrying a child and giving birth is a natural one, yes, but the reasons behind each woman's desire may be different. Certainly, the wonder of growing life inside you is exciting; but some women desire pregnancy to prove their womanhood or to hold together a shaky marriage. Some men feel the need to prove their manhood by impregnating their wives. Exactly what—and how much—does a pregnancy mean to you?

The emotional satisfaction of sharing the birth/ breastfeeding experience and the bonding of parent and child at birth. Do you believe these are necessary to form a strong relationship with a child?

The chance to be a parent. Maybe what upsets you most of all is the thought that you may never have the opportunity to share in this very special, life-long relationship.

Control. It's difficult to hand so much of your life over to doctors, lawyers, adoption agencies—even to the Lord—when you've always been able to handle things in the past. Are you most upset by the loss of this independence?

You might even want to add to this list; maybe you've sacrificed self-esteem, a healthy sex life, a constructive marriage, or even a thriving career. Each of these losses is a disappointment in itself, but deciding which one hurts the very most can help you to choose a wise plan of action.

Step Two: Generate Alternatives

Once you've decided what you really want, you can generate alternative ways of reaching that goal. Sit down with pencil and paper and brainstorm. Write down any possibilities, no matter how farfetched, contradictory, or silly they sound. For instance, if your ultimate goal is to become parents, your options might be:

- wait for a miracle
- artificial insemination with husband's sperm

- artificial insemination with donor's sperm
- private adoption
- apply for agency adoption
- intrauterine insemination
- in vitro fertilization
- GIFT (gamete intrafallopian transfer)

Step Three: Evaluate the Alternatives

Of course, some alternatives you'll strike automatically (those that are obviously immoral or illegal). But don't be too quick to rule out options unfamiliar to you. To make the best decision, it's absolutely essential that you evaluate every aspect of each option. This can be done in several ways. You can:

Read everything you can get your hands on about the option: books for lay people and medical personnel, magazine articles from popular magazines and professional journals, pamphlets from organizations that deal with the option, television transcripts—everything. Just be sure you always read with a critical eye; not all materials will support the world view that all life comes from God, that man and woman are created in his image.

Write to every organization and source you can find that can give information about the subject. Here, too, remember that some organizations will have philosophies that are out of sync with a believer's values.

Talk to people who have chosen the alternative you're considering. Ask them why they made the choice, how they made it, if they have any suggestions for you as you struggle with the decision.

Consider your doctor's advice. Of course physicians are not God, but they do have the benefit of medical training and experience. When we consider the extraordinary means used to prolong and preserve life today, some of the extraordinary means used to initiate life are put in perspective. Indeed, medical science is one of the means God gives us for bringing about his will in people's lives. Balance your doctor's recommendations for your best alternative with your own knowledge and convictions.

List the positives and negatives of each option. This is not a new method, and making an important decision is certainly more complex than writing down a list of pros and cons. But it is an important part of investigating all sides of each option.

Equally as important as being objective in your pro/con list is being *subjective* in determining the morality of each option. I would love to be able to take "the Christian stand" on each of these alternatives. If it were that clear, the decision-making process would be much easier, and my husband and I (and thousands of other infertile couples) would have been spared a lot of the agony involved in trying to decide what's best.

But the options cannot be so easily divided into God's way and the world's way. Many Christians differ among themselves as to which alternatives are acceptable and which are not. However, God does offer guidance when it comes to the basic issues which make these options so confounding and controversial. Therefore, it is important to **pray** long, hard, and consistently about which choices are best for you; to **seek spiritual counsel**; and to **meditate** on (not just read) Scripture and apply it to your questions.

Evaluating the Options

When you choose an option, you make a decision to do at least one of five things:

1. Remain childless
2. Adopt
3. Use a substitute method for intercourse
4. Introduce a third party's genes into the conception of a child
5. Allow the manipulation of human embryos

Let's take a look at these options, examine their "morality" in light of what God has to say about the basic principles on which they operate, and list a few of their advantages and disadvantages. Again, feel free to add your own impressions as you read.

Childfree Living

My mother once told me that, had she had severe fertility problems when she was young, she might well have chosen to remain childless (a real tribute to my brother and me, I kidded her). Of course, she doesn't know for sure what she would have done, but I admire her independent thinking. To choose childlessness in the 1950s was a social deviance. If childlessness chose you, you were pitied. But a deliberate decision to remain childfree often branded you as a selfish, rather narcissistic couple.

Then attitudes changed somewhat, and in the 1970s the term "pronatalism" surfaced as "any attitude or policy that is 'pro-birth,' that encourages reproduction, that exalts the role of parenthood."[3] Opponents of pronatalism were upset by couples who were having children, not because they really wanted to be parents but because parenthood was expected of them. These "non-parents" encouraged men and women to evaluate their goals and themselves before they had babies and to consider child-free living as an alternative.

Think about it. Parenthood is God's intention for many people, but he never said a childless marriage cannot be valid or happy. There are ways for a couple to live an enormously fulfilling life without children.

It may seem ironic reading books with titles such as *Childless by Choice*, since we feel the choice has been taken away. Actually it hasn't. We may not be able to have biological children, but there are other ways of becoming parents. What's important is that we not just drift into childlessness without consciously choosing it. Making a decision for or against helps us make the most of any alternative we select. In looking at childlessness, consider:

- social disapproval you might encounter. There are people who think of the childless as self-centered, materialistic, and even a little neurotic. Everywhere you turn (you know this by now) is pressure to reproduce—from the federal government and its income tax deductions for children, to the media and its idyllic, lopsided view of parenthood. Childless couples are not the norm in our society. Be prepared to stand your ground and stick to what's best for you.

- the tradeoff—giving up the parenting and grandparenting experience in exchange for different (but just as valuable) ways of spending your life.

- the extra effort you must make to stay in contact with and understand people who do have children and the generation coming up behind you. This can be done in a variety of ways, but usually it must be done deliberately.

• how your decision affects others, particularly your parents. They may grieve over the absence of grandchildren.

However, also be aware that

• a childfree marriage has limitless potential to be the best possible, since you can focus more attention on each other.

• you can establish long-term relationships with nieces and nephews and other young people—valuable because you can offer your wisdom, affection, and perspective, and maybe more uninterrupted attention than the parents have.

• you can put more energy into your career.

• you could well have more time and stamina to minister to the needs of others as a couple.

Adoption

If only women with unwanted pregnancies could crawl into the hearts of infertile couples—just for a little while—maybe adoption wouldn't be so difficult or take so long. As it is, adoptable babies are harder to find these days due in part to the increased availability of reliable birth control, the social acceptance of single parenthood, and legalized abortion.

Most Christians have no problem dealing with the morality of adoption. (We ourselves are God's adopted children having "received a spirit of adoption as sons by which we cry out 'Abba! Father!'" [Romans 8:15]) Many people do, however, have trouble dealing with the process of adoption. It may be grueling at times, but through your experience with infertility you've already developed some coping skills that will help: patience and unswerving, die-hard persistence. If you're considering adoption, there are a couple of routes you can take.

Agency adoption takes place through agencies licensed by the state. These agencies usually provide counseling for the birth mother and prospective parents; they evaluate the child medically and obtain medical histories of birth parents; they make sure the child is legally free for adoption. Adoption agencies are also required to screen prospective parents carefully. For you, this means providing references from friends, birth certificates, your marriage license, verification of your employment, fingerprints, and maybe financial records. A social worker will visit you in your home to make sure you can safely and comfortably accommodate a child. You may feel as though your entire life is scrutinized from the inside out, and you may resent it from time to time. Just remember, the agency is being choosy for the child's sake.

You can usually find adoption agencies in the Yellow Pages, through your state licensing agency, welfare department, or department of social services, or by asking your doctor. Most adoptions begin with a phone call to one of these places. Be prepared to be told there's a long wait for a baby (two to five years or more), but most will put you on the waiting list.

With **private adoptions** (sometimes called nonagency or independent adoptions), there may be a shorter wait. A private adoption takes place without the assistance of an agency. Instead a doctor, lawyer, friend, or minister acts as the intermediary, telling the couple of a pregnant woman (or a woman who has recently delivered) who has chosen not to keep her baby. If you are considering private adoption, it is essential to hire a lawyer you trust completely, whose reputation is spotless, and ideally who has had experience dealing with independent adoptions. The birth mother in this case will relinquish her child to specific people (you and your spouse). Then, in order to legally adopt the child, you will have to provide many of the same written documents that an agency requires. In addition, a type of home study may be done by a court-appointed representative or designated agency, and you may have to go to court yourself.

Private adoptions are not legal in all states, and even where they are legal the process is usually riskier than agency adoption. Since the child is not legally free for adoption during much of the process, there is a chance that one of the birth parents will have a change of heart and want to keep the child. Furthermore, without good legal counsel, there's a greater chance for conflict when your case comes to court for finalization. In private adoption, too, there is no one to counsel the couple or the birth mother about the emotional risks of adoption. However, private adoption usually yields faster results with less red tape. Many couples have gone this route successfully and would do so again for a second child.

Black market adoption is an illegal business in which the intermediary is paid for the baby, not just for the service performed. To be sure your private adoption is not black market, check the reliability of your intermediary and ask for an itemized list of your expenses (lawyer's fee, the birth mother's hospital bills, and travel costs).

If you're thinking about adoption, you might want to join an adoptive parents support group. They can give you much needed emotional support during your search for a child and more information on how the adoption system works.

In looking at this option, it's also wise to consider:

- your infertility. Have you accepted it, come to terms with it? If you haven't, you might want to give yourself more time. If you consider yourself a failure, your adopted child may be a constant reminder of that "failure" instead of a source of joy.

- the possibility that your adopted child might want to seek out his biological parents. Could you accept your child's desire to do this without feeling threatened?

- your willingness to accept outside help. A legal adoption, public or private, involves dependence on other people, whether they be counselors, lawyers, social workers, or courts.

- an adopted child's past. Since most infants available for adoption are children of unwed mothers, it's wise to examine your attitude toward babies born out of wedlock. Some children are also victims of poverty and war. They may have been malnourished or abused. Could you deal with your child's less than ideal past?

- your persistence level. Could you pursue adoption in spite of disappointments, red tape, and long waits? Adoption can be a real test of your commitment.

On the other hand, be aware that:

- the child would be no more biologically yours

than your spouse's. You would both be starting on equal biological ground and wouldn't
have to deal with emotional complications
that sometimes arise when the child is related
genetically to only one parent.

- rather than adding to an already exploding
population, you would be giving the gift of
family in its finest sense to a child who needs
you very much.

- though adoption itself will not resolve your
infertility, someday—after all that waiting,
the frustration, and many prayers—you will
be parents at last.

- even a couple's biological baby does not automatically fit in upon arrival home from the
hospital. The arrival of a child—regardless of
how he came to be yours—always requires
quite an adjustment. Remember that families
are made, not born.

Substitutes for Intercourse

Artificial Insemination by Husband (AIH)

Intrauterine Insemination (IUI)

Gamete Intrafallopian Transfer (GIFT)

These options are generally less controversial than
others, mainly because only the husband's sperm and the
wife's egg are involved. If fertilization occurs, it does so in
the wife's fallopian tubes, so there is no tampering with or
disposal of embryos.

Some Christians feel uneasy with these options because they are so "unnatural." God designed our bodies to

create children through intercourse; these methods bypass the lovemaking and get right to the mechanics.

True, God's original plan did not include being inseminated through a catheter; but faulty reproductive organs were not in his original plan for our bodies either, any more than nearsightedness, hearing loss, or gall stones. Yet just as we wear glasses, use hearing aids, and have surgery to help ourselves, surely we have the same option to do what we can to help our reproductive organs function as God intended.

Artificial Insemination with Husband's Sperm (AIH). As a teenager in Indiana, I thought artificial insemination was only for cattle. Little did I know that some day I'd consider it for myself!

Artificial insemination is a relatively simple procedure where semen is collected, placed into a syringe, and squirted into the woman's vagina near the cervix. She then lies on her back for about thirty minutes to allow the semen to liquefy and the sperm to begin swimming toward the egg. There are two basic types of artificial insemination: with the husband's sperm (AIH) and with the sperm of a donor (AID).

AIH can be helpful when the husband's sperm count is low, with poor motility; he is unable to maintain an erection; he suffers from retrograde ejaculation; he cannot ejaculate during intercourse; or if a woman has antibodies to her husband's sperm or has a chronic cervical infection.

The success rate for AIH is not particularly high—around 20 percent, at best, per insemination—and it may seem a bit mechanical, since it involves the doctor coming between a man (and his sperm) and his wife (and her egg). However, it is a viable option for some couples.

Intrauterine Insemination (IUI). This is yet another option for couples with problems such as low sperm counts and motility, cervical mucus which kills sperm, or unexplained infertility. In this procedure, a semen sample (from a donor or the husband) is collected and "washed" several times by placing the sperm in a special medium and spinning the mixture on a centrifuge. (Washing is necessary since injection of the seminal fluid directly into the uterus may cause expulsion of the semen, painful cramps, even fainting.) The washed sperm are then inserted directly into the uterus where they won't have to swim quite so far to meet an egg. In 1987, the success rate for IUI was about 15 percent per attempt for the proper candidates.

Gamete Intrafallopian Transfer (GIFT). GIFT has been statistically more successful than in vitro fertilization (IVF); however, a woman must have at least one fallopian tube open to qualify for the procedure. Participants are those who have unexplained infertility, low sperm counts, or cervical or immunological conditions that affect fertility.

With GIFT, as with IVF, the woman is given fertility drugs to encourage the development of several eggs. She is then anesthetized, and the eggs are harvested via laparoscope. Meanwhile, the husband collects a semen sample, it is washed, and then the eggs and sperm are placed separately into a catheter and injected into the woman's fallopian tube.

Introduction of a Third Party's Genes

Artificial Insemination by Donor (AID)

Donor Eggs

Surrogate Mothers

God told Abram his descendants would number as many as the stars in the sky. But we all know how hard it is to wait—especially when God takes what seems to be an inordinate amount of time to fulfill a promise. Finally, Sarai told Abram to have intercourse with Hagar, her maid, to produce a much wanted heir. But once Hagar was obviously pregnant, Sarai regretted her decision and treated Hagar so harshly she fled (Genesis 16:1-6).

When a third party's genetic material helps produce a child for a couple, more than mere biology must be reckoned with. When egg and sperm donors are used, the spouse who is "left out" biologically must come to terms with this peculiar type of exclusion. With AID, the wife carries another man's child; with donor eggs, the wife carries another woman's child; a surrogate mother carries the husband's child for the couple.

Involving another person this way can create physical and emotional ties and complications that may last a lifetime. Some Christians reject these options for that reason; others believe the rewards outweigh the difficulties.

Though Abram and Sarai were acting according to the custom of the day, this arrangement wasn't God's original best for them. Be sure you and your spouse make the Lord himself your third party before enlisting anyone else.

Artificial Insemination by Donor (AID). AID is more complicated than AIH. This procedure is generally used if the husband's sperm count is zero or so low that he cannot impregnate his wife, or if there's a risk of passing on a genetic disease. This type of insemination follows the same course as AIH with one critical difference that may exclude this as an option: the semen comes from an anonymous male, usually a member of the hospital's medical staff. Many doctors do their best to match the donor's physical characteristics (hair, eye and skin color, build) with the husband's. However, with the introduction of a third party's genes into the wife's system come some emotion-laden issues the couple must face. Those who consider AID must deal with:

- the genetic "inequality" of marriage partners: this child would have only one parent's genes.

- the husband's feelings about the whole procedure. He must be able to admit his inability to impregnate his wife and accept the fact that she is carrying another man's biological child. Some people consider AID adultery, even though there is no emotional union between the genetic parents.

- the child's legal status. Not all states have laws that deal with the rights of AID children. To protect these rights, attorney Lori Andrews suggests you take steps to ensure that, under the law, your child is the offspring of your marriage and that you grant rights to your child by name.

- what you would tell your family, your friends, and your child. If you decided to stay mum, how long could a secret like this be kept? What if your child developed an illness that required the medical history of both parents? On the other hand, if you decided to tell your child about her conception, how much would she understand? AID is physically more complicated than adoption. Would your child have negative feelings about being different in this way?

- inbreeding. What happens if a man and woman fall in love and decide to marry, only to find that they're half-brother and half-sister? It may be improbable, but it is possible, especially if a doctor uses a local donor to inseminate more than one woman.

- the abuse of AID. With the ability to inseminate a woman with sperm from a donor come some rather frightening possibilities. Some people equate AID with "sperm bank mentality"—that is, the ability to "order up" a certain kind of child with designated physical features and a high I.Q. Is it our right to try to design a "perfect baby" for ourselves?

Although it is impossible for the Christian to lay aside these ethical question concerning genetic engineering, be aware that:

- statistically fewer birth defects occur in AID babies than in the general population, since the donors are carefully screened.

- both husband and wife can participate in the miracle of pregnancy and delivery. The wife can breastfeed the baby. In short, the child would be under your influence from the moment he was born.

- at least one of you could contribute to the child's genetic makeup. Some people consider AID "half an adoption."

- AID has a relatively high success rate: pregnancy results in about 70 percent of women who are inseminated.[4]

- the wait may not be long. Most women who are going to get pregnant by AID do so within about six months.

Donor Eggs. In 1984, Australian scientists announced the birth of the world's first "donor egg" baby. In this case, the egg was retrieved from one woman (the donor) and placed in a petri dish with the husband's sperm. The egg was fertilized and placed into the uterus of the wife, where it implanted.

With this procedure, the couple can share the joys of pregnancy, and the child will carry the genes of one parent. However, finding a suitable egg donor may be difficult since retrieving an egg is much more complicated than collecting sperm. Timing must be perfect for this procedure since the donor must be ovulating when the wife's uterus is ready to accept a pregnancy. In addition, the couple must face many of the same concerns as those who choose to try artificial insemination by donor.

Surrogate Mothers (Third-party pregnancy). "All you're doing," claims a housewife from Illinois, "is transferring the pain from one woman to another, from a woman who is in pain from her infertility to a woman who has to give up her baby."[5]

That's one woman's view of surrogate motherhood, and certainly not a complete view. The well-publicized case of Mary Beth Whitehead and the Sterns in New Jersey demonstrates the agony of involving a third party as a means to resolve infertility.

Most couples who choose this option are in their thirties or forties, and financially comfortable. The wife may be unable to ovulate or carry a child to term, or she may be afraid of passing on a genetic disease to her child. The couple may be considered too old by most adoption agencies.

The arrangement is usually made through a lawyer or agency that specializes in matching surrogates and prospective parents. The surrogate is artificially inseminated with the husband's sperm, agreeing in a contract that if she gets pregnant, she will surrender the child to the husband and wife and not fight for the child's custody. For this, the couple pays her medical expenses and a fee for the mother herself.

Why would any woman want to bear a child for another couple? Some women enjoy being pregnant. Some feel that bearing a child for an infertile couple is giving the ultimate gift of life to a wife and husband. Some are trying to resolve guilt over a past abortion or resolve their feelings about another birth-related trauma. For many, however, money is the motivator. Consider:

- the cost. The surrogate's fee is normally at least $10,000. By the time the baby is legally yours, most likely you will have spent $25,000 or more.

- the law. At this point, the law in most states makes no specific provision for the surrogate arrangement. There are no guarantees that your contract will hold up in court. What if the surrogate changes her mind and decides to keep the baby? What rights does the father have? It's important to check out your state's laws regarding surrogacy, artificial insemination, adoption, stepparenting, and related areas. It's also essential to hire a good lawyer, although lawyers with experience in this area may be hard to find.

- the child. Would you tell him about his unusual conception? Would you agree to stay in contact with his birth mother? Would his mother be allowed to visit periodically? What would his feelings toward his mother be if he learned she was paid to conceive, deliver, and relinquish him to you?

- society's attitude. AID at least gives the pretense (to outsiders) of a traditional pregnancy. When you hire a surrogate mother, however, few secrets can be kept. How would you handle the negative reactions of friends and relatives?

- your feelings about "baby selling." Is this a form of it? What's the difference between paying for a baby and paying someone to carry your baby?

On the other hand, be aware that:

- the baby would have the father's genes.

- since women are usually screened for genetic or acquired diseases and normally provide information about their personalities, health, and physical characteristics, there's an excellent chance of having a bright, healthy baby.

- the baby would be yours from the beginning. She would have no history of being abused or traumatized, provided there is no scenario such as the Whitehead case.

- you would probably know more about the child's genetic history than that of an adopted child.

- medically, the procedure is simple, if it just involves artificial insemination (rather than embryo transfer).

Manipulation of Human Embryos

Embryo Transfer

In Vitro Fertilization (IVF)

In considering IVF and embryo transfer, the biggest dilemma most Christians face is deciding whether the manipulation of human embryos is moral.

Do keep in mind as you investigate such processes that in the midst of all the variables involved, there is one constant: life does begin at conception. Dr. Paul Fowler, in his book *Abortion: Toward an Evangelical Consensus*, challenges the view that life is a process of growth (from one cell to two to four and so on into that of a full-fledged "person"). Rather, life is an event that begins with a fertilized egg.[6]

In Psalm 139, David recognizes the significance of his own life before birth:

For Thou didst form my inward parts;
Thou didst weave me in my mother's womb.

. . . .

My frame was not hidden from Thee,
When I was made in secret,
And skillfully wrought in the depths of the earth.
Thine eyes have seen my unformed substance;
And in Thy book they were all written,
The days that were ordained for me,
When as yet there was not one of them.

(vv. 13, 15-16)

Human embryos are not "potential persons"; they are human life and should be treated with the utmost care and respect.

Embryo Transfer. Some women, rather than lending their entire bodies for nine months, have participated in embryo transfer in return for a payment of about $250. Here a woman is given ovulation-inducing drugs to stimulate the production of several eggs. She then consents to being inseminated with the husband's sperm. If she becomes pregnant, the fertilized egg or eggs are flushed out through a catheter and examined to make sure that normal cell division has taken place. If this is the case, the fertilized eggs are placed in a special transfer fluid and introduced by a catheter into the wife's uterus at a time in her cycle when her body is receptive to a pregnancy. Candidates for embryo transfer include women who can't ovulate, those who threaten to pass on a genetic disease, or those for whom IVF has failed. As you think about embryo transfer, consider:

- your views on abortion. Remember that the fertilized egg is removed from the biological mother's uterus. Granted, it is not removed in order to destroy life—but most embryos do not survive the transfer.

- the child. As with AID, you must decide what to tell the child about her conception.

- the legal status of the child. Would the wife need to adopt the baby? Would the donor have any rights to the child?

On the other hand, be aware that

- embryo transfer is less costly than IVF.

- the couple can experience pregnancy and delivery together.
- the procedure is relatively simple; there is no surgery involved.

In Vitro Fertilization. I've always found the term "test tube baby" distasteful, mainly because of the Frankenstein picture it paints in uninformed minds. It pays to find out exactly what in vitro fertilization involves.

Briefly, the process entails giving the woman fertility drugs—sometimes clomiphene citrate, sometimes Pergonal, sometimes a mixture of both (it varies from doctor to doctor). This drug treatment is included in the $4,000 to $5,000 fee for the whole procedure, and the risks are minimal as long as the woman is carefully monitored. The fertility drugs stimulate (and make it easier to predict) ovulation. Frequent blood tests and ultrasounds are used to predict the exact time. Then when ovulation is imminent, the doctor performs a laparoscopy to prick the ovaries and remove all the ripe eggs by aspiration through a tube.

As an alternative to laparoscopy, vaginal egg retrieval is now being used for some women. For this procedure, ultrasound helps determine where the ripe follicles are located. Then a long needle attached to a probe is gently pushed through the wall of the vagina and into the ovary at the site of the mature follicle.

When the eggs are collected, they are allowed to mature in a special medium. Meanwhile, the sperm are being washed in the same type of medium. Then each egg is placed in a separate petri dish along with some sperm— and cheered on.

Usually the eggs that are going to be fertilized will be in twenty-four hours. These embryos are allowed to grow a few days. Then they are drawn into a thin tube which is inserted into the uterus through the vagina and cervix. Ideally, at least one will implant and yield a pregnancy and a healthy baby.

In vitro fertilization candidates are typically women who can ovulate but have damaged or missing fallopian tubes; women with husbands who have low sperm counts or motility; or women whose husbands' sperm are incapable of living in the cervix. IVF has also been performed for couples whose infertility remains unexplained.

If you're thinking that IVF might be an option for you, consider:

- the cost, which is usually $4,000 to $5,000, but can run higher. This doesn't include transportation to the nearest clinic, accommodations, and food.

- the high anxiety the whole procedure creates. The surgery, blood tests, ultrasounds, hormone injections, and your dependence on your doctor are all likely to take their toll on your emotional health.

- your deepest feelings about the morality of it all. Some people argue that tampering with human embryos is "playing God," especially when the question of the extra embryos comes up. Typically, if fertility drugs are administered, the physician retrieves about five eggs; but doctors have harvested as many as seventeen. If more were fertilized than the uterus could possibly carry to term upon implantation, how would your doctor handle them? Would he introduce all embryos back into the uterus anyway . . . introduce a few and freeze the rest . . . introduce a few and destroy the rest? What are the rights of the embryo?

- the low success rate. After your time, money, and emotions are spent, you may be left with bills and no baby. For 1987, the pregnancy rate per laparoscopy was 30 percent at best, and often much lower. Eggs may not be retrieved; if retrieved, they may not fertilize; if fertilized, they may not implant. And about a third of the women whose embryos do implant miscarry the fetus in the first trimester.

But also be aware that:

- genetically, an IVF baby would be 100 percent yours as a couple.

- both partners could share the pregnancy and birth experience.

- though very involved, this procedure presents a tremendous opportunity for the right candidates. (Be sure your infertility is properly diagnosed before you are put on a waiting list.)

- thus far, there is no evidence to suggest that careful handling of the embryo causes chromosomal damage. Most IVF babies have been born perfectly healthy.

- this procedure is a partnership. To some it may seem cold and harsh—but even with no bodies coming together, the process is still a

team effort between husband and wife. Sometimes the husband is allowed to give hormone
injections, and often he is with his wife when
the fertilized eggs are introduced into her
uterus.

So many choices to make and ethical matters to consider—it makes my head ache just to think about them all.
What's best for me? My spouse? What does God want us to
do? Chances are your head is aching too as you consider
alternatives and the possibilities generated by them.

Even fertile people have a hard time deciding how
they feel. One congressman from Tennessee, the father of
four, acknowledged his own ambivalence toward current
trends in creating new life, but then conceded that "the
touching search for children may justify a great many
things that make others of us who are more fortunate
uncomfortable."[7]

Consider Sarah and Abraham; Hannah and Elkanah;
Rachel and Jacob; Elizabeth and Zacharias. Surely from
their stories and God's instructions to "be fruitful and
multiply" (Genesis 1:28) we can conclude that the search
for children is at least justifiable, if not worth pain and
sacrifice.

Just how much does the search for children justify?
Your answer will most certainly require a thorough analysis—physically and spiritually—of the alternatives.

Step Four: Choose an Alternative

This could be the most difficult step of all, but chances
are, if you've investigated your options, you've probably
emerged with some basic ideas about what you'd like to
try. The process of choosing one will involve:

Common sense. If your sperm count is zero, obviously AIH will not help you. If you're over forty, adopting a healthy infant through an agency might be next to impossible. The causes of your infertility, your age, the size of your savings account, your emotional reserves—these and many other factors force you to use common sense in choosing and eliminating alternatives.

Your desires. If you've studied adoption thoroughly and still don't feel good about the arrangement, don't be afraid to admit those negative feelings. Don't feel guilty about them, either. Adoption isn't for everyone; neither is in vitro fertilization or childfree living. Bring your deepest feelings to the surface and let them help you make a decision.

Compromise. What if your basic desires and your spouse's are different? Then compromise is in order. Let's say your husband's sperm count is low and nothing can seem to improve it. He may be ready for in vitro fertilization. You, however, feel uneasy about a third party handling your embryos outside of your body. Trying GIFT may be a suitable compromise.

Short-range goals. You might want to outline a long-range plan that includes short-range goals. For instance, you might want to try IUI, but your emotional and financial reserves are exhausted right now. In that case, you may decide to stop infertility treatment for three months (make sure your goals, long and short, are specific) and then try IUI for six cycles. Or you might decide in the long range to adopt a child. In the short range, you could plan to call three adoption agencies and read one book on adoption next week.

This kind of planning will not only help you reach your destination; it will also make the journey there more productive.

Step Five: Commit Yourself Wholeheartedly

At some point you are bound to have mixed emotions about any alternatives, so don't be surprised if you find yourself concerned about your ability to love an adopted child or, while lying on the table in your doctor's office, a little turned off by the "unnatural" procedure of artificial insemination. Ambivalence is part of nearly every decision you make; but if your dominant feelings about the procedure are positive, you've probably chosen well. The key, then, once you've decided on a path to take is to dedicate yourself to it wholeheartedly.

If you perceive adoption as second best, then it will be; if childlessness chooses you and you resign yourself to it as a life of emptiness, it will be.

Of course, some options may not yield the results you want. Your attempts may continue to be unsuccessful, and you might want to step back and reevaluate. That's fine. Take a breather, reappraise, then repeat the decision-making process. But don't be discouraged at the thought of starting all over again—because you're not. If you've given this investigation your best shot the first time around, you'll find that you've now become more knowledgeable about your options, better acquainted with yourself, and skilled enough with the procedure to apply it to other kinds of decisions you must make.

I am not a wise person by nature, but I've always felt I had enough emotional and intellectual strength to pull me through a decent-sized crisis. However, by the time we were knee-deep into infertility, I was convinced there was not only a hole in my heart but several in my head as well.

I can't honestly tell you that those holes don't still exist: that the ones in my head never lead me to poor choices or the one in my heart never hurts. I know now, though, that the smartest decision I can ever make is the one to fill them all up with God himself.

> *But if any of you lacks wisdom, let him ask of God, who gives to all men generously and without reproach, and it will be given to him*
>
> (James 1:5).

Chapter 10, Notes

1. Merle Bombardieri, *The Baby Decision* (New York: Rawson, Wade Publishers, 1981), 6-7.

2. Patricia Johnston, *An Adopter's Advocate* (Fort Wayne, Ind.: Perspectives Press, 1984), 25.

3. Ellen Peck and Judith Senderowitz, eds., *Pronatalism: The Myth of Mom and Apple Pie* (New York: Thomas Y. Crowell, 1974), 9.

4. William W. Beck, "Artificial Insemination and Semen Preservation," *Infertility in the Male*, ed. Larry I. Lipshultz and Stuart S. Howards (New York: Churchill Livingstone, 1983), 386.

5. Barbara Kantrowitz et al., "Who Keeps 'Baby M'?" *Newsweek*, 19 January 1987, 46.

6. Paul Fowler, *Abortion: Toward an Evangelical Consensus* (Portland, Ore.: Multnomah Press, 1987), 49.

7. Otto Friedrich, "A Legal, Moral, Social Nightmare," *Time*, 10 September 1984, 56.

How many times have we prayed for a child? I'm afraid to count—because that's the number of times God has turned us down. I'm so frustrated with his negative answers that sometimes I don't pray at all. I just sit—while a thousand questions swim around in my head. Has he forgotten us or what?

11

God, Have You Forgotten Us?

The first time I remember praying was one hot July night when I was ten years old. My father had been sick for about a week—with food poisoning, the doctor thought. I hated to see him so ill. He tried to chuckle and joke around, but even I could tell he just wasn't himself. So naturally at bedtime I was moved to pray, "Dear God, please make my Daddy well." Then with childlike faith, confident my prayers would be answered, I rolled over and promptly fell asleep. It was Tuesday.

On Wednesday he looked a little better. The doctor came out for a visit and announced that he was much improved. That night I happily thanked the Lord for that good report, and prayed, "Dear God, keep working on him till he feels good." And again, knowing my prayers were heard and answered, I rolled over and fell asleep.

On Thursday my Daddy died. I didn't know what to say to God then. A kind woman at church assured me that God did answer my prayer—just not the way I expected. My father was very well indeed, she said, now that he was with Jesus. I gratefully accepted her comforting words; nevertheless, for a long time after that, when I'd pray for my brother to get home safely or for my mother to feel better soon, I'd P.S. my prayers with "You know what I mean." I really was afraid God would give me another trick answer.

His omnipotence became real to me then in a rather frightening way. I perceived him as an unpredictable force, striking who-knows-where next. "God is love," my Sunday school teachers told me. But what kind of love, I wondered, snatches a kid's father away before she's finished growing up? And what kind of love, I wondered years later, would deprive a man and a woman of the children they ache to have and hold?

Though I like to think I've matured spiritually since I was ten, our infertility resurrected many of my childhood questions about the nature of God and prayer. "Why should I pray to him," I'd ask myself, "if he's not going to give me what I want? Is there some secret to getting an affirmative answer? If so, what am I doing wrong? How should I pray? How can I be expected to converse with someone I can't see or hear?"

We have too many questions and not enough answers, it seems. We beg for a baby. We feel guilty about being so "selfish," but we can't help ourselves, so we begin begging again. Then we get angry and frustrated when God doesn't give us a child. How do we approach an all-powerful God anyway? Especially when we're angry and baffled by the way he operates.

Personally, my prayer life is most satisfying when I stop to remind myself of the nature of God. I certainly must acknowledge his omnipotence, omniscience, and omnipresence. I know him as my creator and my lifeguard, the One who gave me life and the One who sustains it. But when I come to God in prayer, I feel him most definitely as my Father. And every good father invites questions from his children.

Why Should I Pray?

The Bible says that "your Father knows what you need, before you ask Him" (Matthew 6:8). Why in the world, then, does God want us to tell him what he already knows?

This verse makes little sense if we think of prayer as a way to transmit a Christmas list (no surprises, please) to heaven. But God is not Santa Claus, and prayer is not merely a string of requests with instructions on how they should be answered.

Prayer is interaction—dialogue—between God and humans. It is a way for us to establish a loving relationship with God. Think of it like this: as you were growing up, why did you talk to your earthly father? Just to get something you wanted? Of course not. Your conversations probably took many forms: discussing the day's events; asking questions; expressing affection, hostility, gratitude. Naturally you made your share of requests, but that wasn't the sole reason for communicating with each other. The exchange between father and child ideally helped you to understand each other, to grow to love each other. For that reason, God wants us to talk with him, to stay in touch.

We all know what happens when we stop communicating with a friend or parent. It doesn't take long before we feel we have nothing in common any more, nothing to talk about. This is the last thing God wishes for us in our bond with him. Yet often it is the first part of that bond to deteriorate, mainly because we come to prayer with a "give me what I want or I'm not talking" attitude. Try to remember that establishing that loving relationship is all-important. Yes, God knows what we need before we ask, and he's always there, ready to talk about it. But we must pick up (and keep up) our end of the line to hold a conversation.

Sounds fairly simple, yes? Well, not always, especially when you have a request that's burning in your heart—a request that's been repeatedly denied. I prayed for a baby so long and so hard that I began to think something was very wrong with my prayers. Maybe you're asking some of the same questions that troubled me.

How Should I Pray?

Pray daily. This takes some self-discipline, because our tendency is to put prayer on the back burner till we find time for it, and that block of time rarely materializes. We get up too late in the morning, we're too tired at night, and too busy during the day. But we must take time for conversation with God each day if we expect to learn from him and hear him when he answers.

Many people find that early morning prayer is best, since most households are quiet then. Try getting up, bathing, and getting dressed first. (Attempting to pray while you're still lying in bed is asking for trouble!) This way you'll be awake, and your day will be off to its finest possible start.

Pray honestly. As a player of great games, I've also participated in a few that aren't so great. One I indulge in occasionally is called "I've Got a Secret." It goes like this: When something is really bugging me, Ben will ask, "What's wrong?" and I'll say, "Nothing." Then he'll say, "Come on, what's on your mind?" and I'll say, "Really, it's nothing." Then he'll say, "Why the big secret? Just tell me what's the matter." Then I'll say, "I told you, nothing is wrong." Then he has the nerve to believe me, and he drops the matter. Meanwhile, I'm eating myself alive inside, dying to tell him how I really feel. Pretty silly, isn't it?

Yet too often we play the same game with God. We try to pretend nothing's wrong; we come to him with what should be in our hearts ("Bless Mary and Bill and their new baby"), but we feel too guilty or afraid to tell him what's really in our hearts ("But Lord, I don't want to smile and be happy for other people. I don't feel like being so controlled and so good. What I'd really like to do is run outside and scream, then run in the house and break dishes. And to tell you the truth, I don't really feel like I love you much right now").

God is not fooled by the brave front we present to the rest of the world. I find it helpful to begin my prayers as honestly as I can, admitting my negative feelings when they come. Only when I bring them to him can he help me deal with them.

Pray specifically. It's certainly "safer" to pray in sweeping generalities ("Make all the sick people well, all the starving people full, and all the infertile couples fertile") than it is to be specific in our requests. But since the purpose of prayer is to establish two-way communication with God, we need to hear his response—and we tend not to search for answers to mouthful prayers as we do for bite-sized ones.

For instance, instead of praying for help through your entire investigation, you might narrow your focus and ask God for courage when you go in for a laparoscopy; ask him to guide the doctor's hands. Ask him to ease your embarrassment when you deliver a semen sample in front of a roomful of people. When your sperm count comes in at one million per cc, ask him to remind you that your masculinity and your sperm count aren't directly proportional. Then look for specific answers to your specific prayers. You'll find them.

Over and over in the Bible, Jesus commands us to ask.[1] He set the example himself in the Model Prayer by asking for something as specific as daily bread (Matthew 6:11). In doing so, Jesus showed us that God invites requests from his children; he wants us to ask and he wants to give us everything we need.

"But," you might say, "I've asked him so many times for a baby, and he continually says no." This can be frustrating, but think for a minute again about your earthly father: he, too, probably invited your requests. But did he give you everything you asked for? Why not?

Pray with an open heart and mind. Everything we want may not be everything we need. What we are requesting may not be good for us right now. There's a fine line between asking God to fill our needs and dictating exactly how we want him to answer our prayers. I certainly can't tell anyone what to pray for, but I know that frequently we only have eyes for one certain answer. And when God doesn't deliver in that manner right away, we get upset and feel that our prayers are unheard. Then we quit praying for a while and lose touch with God.

That's why it's so important for us to come to prayer with a heart and mind open to God's way of functioning. I find it helpful in my prayers to concentrate on asking God to fill my need, rather than prescribing a remedy myself. For instance, at one point while writing chapter 9 of this book, I hit a real slump. I was discouraged, tired; I needed some feedback that I wasn't getting. I was tempted to pray for my editor to call with good news and extravagant praise for my writing, but this time I asked God for encouragement—and I left the method up to him. My editor never called, but my encouragement came in the form of a letter and a phone call I made myself!

Praying this way is the first step toward learning to pray in Jesus' name. In John 14:14, Jesus says, "If you ask Me anything in My name, I will do it." This would be easy enough if all we had to do was tack the phrase "in Jesus' name" to the end of our prayers. But it does mean more than that. Praying in Jesus' name is praying as Jesus would: requesting things of God, yes, but wanting more than anything else for God's will to be done (as Jesus did in Gethsemane). This is tough to swallow unless we realize that asking for God's will does not mean putting chains on ourselves; it's not grimly resigning ourselves to a life of restrictions. It's not jail. Actually, it's quite the opposite. The more receptive we are to God's will, the more freedom we experience as we allow him to work his best into our lives.

Does this mean that it's too selfish to pray specifically for a baby? I don't think so. If you stay close to God and feel led to pray that way, go ahead. Families are certainly a part of his plan for mankind. However, be careful of prayers like this: "Lord, I'd like you to give me a blonde, blue-eyed baby—a girl. And I want to get pregnant around Christmas because that's such a neat time of year." You're in prayer, not at McDonald's ordering hamburgers.

And what about the times when you just don't know whether you should ask for something? You've prayed for guidance from the Holy Spirit and are still unsure as to whether your prayers are selfish or not. Again, go ahead and ask. And try to keep in mind that when God closes one door, he opens another. What looks like a *no* clears the way for a great big beautiful *yes* in his eyes and in your life.

Pray with an attitude of helplessness. I almost drowned once. I must have been around nine or ten, and I was only in about six feet of lake water. There were two girls a couple hundred feet away sitting on a pier, but aside from them, I was alone. Somehow I had dog paddled my way too far out, and I'll never forget that awful feeling of choking on the water that filled my mouth and nose. Every now and then I surfaced for a breath, but I couldn't stay above the water. I kicked, flailed, and managed to squeak a "Help!" to the people on the pier. They just sat there. I struggled some more, but the more I fought it, the deeper I sank. Finally, someone who was already in the water saw me and dragged me over to safety. Like a dead fish, I flopped onto the boards of the pier, where one of the girls asked me, "Are you all right?" "Yeah," I said weakly. But inside I was furious. "Of course not, you nitwit," I thought. "I was out there drowning and you just sat here!"

If only I had realized that the water I thought was killing me could have saved me. If only I had relaxed enough to float, the water which surrounded me would have held me, sustained me, and kept me out of trouble. But I just wouldn't let it.

We're so like that with God. He has the power to hold us up if we'll relax and trust him. Instead, so often we insist on doing all the worrying, all the struggling, refusing to admit our helplessness. We may feel weak, but our actions show that we are determined, too many times, to tame circumstances beyond our control. I just celebrated my thirty-fifth birthday, and I battle the temptation to worry about my age in regard to childbearing, about how my time clock is ticking away, about how a woman's fertility drops after age thirty, about how my peak fertility was at least ten years ago—all things I cannot control.

I must constantly remind myself that my best prayers come when I admit to God my helplessness in these areas. I cannot develop a loving relationship with a Father I do not trust or with whom I insist on vying for power. It's only when I pray with this attitude of helplessness that I open myself up to his help.

Pray with your eyes open for communication blocks. It always bothered me when people would tell me that maybe my prayers weren't answered because there was some sin in my life. The image of a God who would remove himself from me because I had sinned made me very uncomfortable.

It's true that God hates sin in any form; but when we sin, *we* step back from *him*. He doesn't stop loving us or helping us, but he will not force himself on us. If we've moved away from him, naturally our relationship with him is distorted.

I loved suckers when I was little, but I hated running clear to the kitchen to throw the sticks away, so I found a convenient depository for them—behind my parents' full-length bedroom mirror. Of course they eventually found the sticks and confronted my brother and me. "I didn't do it . . . honest," he said. And since he was older, I figured he knew all the best answers for threatening questions, so I too said, "I didn't do it . . . honest!" My father punished neither of us, but all day long I was an emotional wreck. I avoided him, and when I absolutely had to speak to him, I made small talk; I was nervous and jumpy. That afternoon, Daddy came into my room to ask me something totally unrelated to the crime. Before he could say a word, I threw up my hands and yelled, "I didn't do it, honest!" I think somehow this tipped him off.

Later in the evening, he called me over to his lap and whispered, "Why don't you tell Mom that you put the sucker sticks behind the mirror?" Hoover Dam broke, and I cried tears of relief, mostly. I admitted what I'd done, and though I still had to clean up the mess I'd made, my relationship with my father was right again—and that's what really mattered to me.

That's what our primary concern should be: a right relationship with God. When we knowingly do something we shouldn't or harbor ill feelings against someone, we naturally tend to avoid God, and our conversation is indeed small talk—superficial communication at best.

It's nice to know that we can come to God—even sit in his lap, if you will—and he'll quietly show us what needs to be corrected. Once we sincerely admit our wrong-doings, we open our communication lines with him again. This is so important if we expect to hear the answers to our prayers.

How Can I Listen for God's Answers?

Picture this: You feel awful. You're in terrible pain, so you make an appointment to see the doctor. When you finally get into the office, the doctor asks you what's wrong. You spend quite a long time explaining all your problems. Then when you're finished talking—before the doctor has a chance to open his mouth—you promptly get up and leave!

O. Hallesby, in his book *Prayer*, compares this scenario to our prayer lives. How often we spill out our requests and complaints to God, then leave him without listening to what he has to say. "We go out," says Hallesby, "just as we came in."[2] Frustrated. Angry. Disappointed. Confused. Wondering why our prayers aren't answered.

But our prayers are answered. Maybe we need to fine-tune our listening skills:

Be still. For some of us, this is the ultimate challenge! Try building a period of silence into your prayer time. You may want to place it at the beginning, asking God to clear your head of distractions (and maybe drowsiness). You might be more comfortable ending your prayers with silence, asking God to direct your thoughts, to show you which direction he wants you to take. You may incorporate it somewhere in the middle. Or you may want to have periods of silence in all these places. Whatever you decide, just make sure that you use this time to concentrate on listening—and you may find that

> As you cease the need to scream, shout, demand, the very peace and quiet you experience blends into the stillness of God's Presence. Then watch out! You will think thoughts that you have not thought before. The silence you cultivate becomes the medium of fresh wisdom from the Creator.[3]

Look for God's answers in different forms. Many times I've wished that God would answer my prayers by writing a note, tying it to a rock, and throwing it through my window. At least I'd have no doubt about who was sending it! The truth is, God has many ways of speaking to us. He can direct our thoughts, change physical events, open and close doors. And he speaks most clearly through the Bible. To help you find God's direction, Dandi Dailey Knorr suggests that you write down commands you find as you study the Bible; then use these commands as guidelines for what you should pray and for finding God's answers.[4]

God also uses people to answer prayers. He can speak encouragement through caring friends, offer help through authors of books, and heal through the skill and knowledge of good physicians. And we ourselves can contribute to the answers of our own prayers as we take the initiative to educate ourselves about infertility and seek the support of others.

You might want to keep a prayer notebook listing in one column your requests and the date, in another God's answer, and in a third column his answering medium. This can help you remember how he's answered your prayers in the past and give you some guidance for listening now and in the future.

Be careful to distinguish your emotions from God's voice. Since God does speak in so many ways, this can be difficult. A good way to keep your ears tuned to his wavelength is to make time for Bible study along with your daily prayers. The more time you spend learning about him, the better you get to know him and the easier it is to distinguish his voice from all others. Our trouble is that sometimes we listen only to sounds we want to hear.

I remember one December a couple of years ago, Ben and I were lying quietly in bed when he suddenly said, "This is it!" "What is?" I sat straight up, thinking he was about to get sick. "This month. This is the month you'll get pregnant. I know it, I feel it. I'm sure of it."

Now you might expect this kind of statement from me—but Ben is an engineer. He thinks in straight lines. He's calm, rational, emotionally controlled.

"Are you sure?" I asked, wanting badly to believe him.

"Absolutely."

And so began a month of positive "signs." Everywhere we turned, the story of Elizabeth and Zacharias kept appearing; I was feeling unusually tired all the time. And one day on the way to school, as I prayed for God's guidance in the whole matter, I pulled up behind a truck whose bumper sticker nearly knocked me over. EXPECT A MIRACLE, it said. I was ecstatic.

Then came the countdown: Day 25, 26, 27, 28—by this time we had the baby's name picked out and the nursery decorating planned. And then came Day 29. I started spotting. "Probably normal in early pregnancy," I told myself. But deep down I was sick with dread. A few hours later, I couldn't deny it any more: those unmistakable cramps, followed by an unmistakable period. I felt beaten, crushed. And I had to tell Ben. And oh, how he wanted a baby—and how he deserved a baby. And how awfully sad and hurt he too would be.

And he was. We were. Our faith was badly shaken. We cried our hearts out to God, and he just didn't seem to care.

Know that God has not deserted you. God hears our prayers. Whether they are requests that are good for us or not, he hears them. And our prayers do not go unanswered; we just misunderstand his answers. He may say yes, he may say no—but he says both because he loves us.

Yet it's so hard, especially during our low times, not to feel as though God has turned his back on us. And it's hard to hear a God who seems so distant, so evasive. But we must remember that rather than being "up there" or nowhere, God never moves from our midst.

> We may ignore, but can nowhere evade, the presence of God. The world is crowded with Him. He walks everywhere incognito. And the incognito is not always hard

to penetrate. The real labor is to remember, to attend. In fact, to come awake. Still more, to remain awake.[5]

C.S. Lewis urges us to perceive the world around us not just as an impersonal sign of God's existence, but rather as a message from him. And just as surely as a touch from a loved one is a message—a hug, a kiss, a nudge that says "I care about you"—so it is when you feel a breeze on your cheek or dive into the ocean, when you taste the tangy sweetness of an apple in the fall or feel the sun warm your skin. God is touching you, sending you a message: "I care about you."

And what about the times when his touch seems harsh? These are the touches of a Father pulling his child out of danger or pushing his child on to new experiences. Through them, too, he sends a message: "I know what will help you grow. Lean on me hard, harder than you ever have before. I love you."

> Don't worry about anything; instead, pray about everything; tell God your needs and don't forget to thank him for his answers. If you do this you will experience God's peace, which is far more wonderful than the human mind can understand. His peace will keep your thoughts and your hearts quiet and at rest as you trust in Christ Jesus (Philippians 4:6-7, TLB).

Why is it infertility always seems worse at night? During the day, I'm surrounded with noise. My mind is occupied and I can hope. But then nighttime comes, and we lie in the darkness, nothing more to say to each other, on pillows wet with our tears, on a bed that used to be a refuge, a place where we would love and dream. But now, this bed, this house—even our love—they all feel so empty tonight . . .

O LORD, My God,

I cried to Thee for help, and Thou didst heal me,
O LORD, Thou hast brought up my soul from Sheol;
Thou hast kept me alive, that I should not go down to the pit.

. . . .

Weeping may last for the night,
But a shout of joy comes in the morning.

. . . .

"Hear, O LORD, and be gracious to me;
LORD, be my helper."
Thou hast turned my laments into dancing;
thou hast stripped off my sackcloth and clothed me with joy,
that my spirit may sing psalms to thee and never cease.
(Psalm 30:2-3, 5, 10-11, NEB)

Here's to joy in the morning. . . .

Chapter 11, Notes _____

1. Matthew 7:7-8; Luke 11:5-13; John 14:13-14; 15:7; 16:23-24.

2. O. Hallesby, *Prayer* (Minneapolis: Augsburg Press, 1931), 95.

3. Wayne Oates, *Nurturing Silence in a Noisy Heart* (Garden City, N. Y.: Doubleday and Company, 1979), 18.

4. Dandi Dailey Knorr, *When the Answer Is No* (Nashville: Broadman Press, 1985), pp. 107-8.

5. C. S. Lewis, *Letters to Malcolm: Chiefly on Prayer* (New York: Harcourt Brace Jovanovich, 1964), 75.

Recommended Reading

Causes and Treatments of Infertility

Bellina, Joseph H. and Josleen Wilson. *You Can Have A Baby.* New York: Crown Publishers, Inc., 1985.

Glass, Robert and Ronald J. Ericsson. *Getting Pregnant in the 1980s.* Berkeley: University of California Press, 1982.

McIlhaney, Joe S., Jr. and Susan Nethery. *1250 Health-Care Questions Women Ask.* Grand Rapids: Baker Book House, 1985.

Silber, Sherman. *How to Get Pregnant.* New York: Charles Scribner's Sons, 1980.

Stangel, John J. *Fertility and Conception: An Essential Guide for Childless Couples.* New York: Paddington Press, 1979.

Miscarriage and Stillbirth

Hanes, Mari and Jack Hayford. *Beyond Heartache.* Wheaton, Ill.: Tyndale House Publishers, 1984.

Pizer, Hank and Christine O'Brien Passlinski. *Coping with Miscarriage.* New York: Dag Hammarskjold Press, 1980.

Vredevelt, Pam W. *Empty Arms*. Portland, Ore.: Multnomah Press, 1984.

Rank, Maureen. *Free to Grieve: Coping with the Trauma of Miscarriage*. Minneapolis: Bethany House, 1985.

Infertility from a Christian Perspective

Anderson, Ann Kiemel. *Taste of Tears, Touch of God*. Nashville: Oliver-Nelson Books, 1984.

Halverson, Kaye and Karen M. Hess. *The Wedded Unmother*. Minneapolis: Augsburg Press, 1980.

Love, Vicky. *Childless Is Not Less*. Minneapolis: Bethany House, 1984.

Stigger, Judith A. *Coping with Infertility*. Minneapolis: Augsburg Press, 1983.

Stout, Martha. *Without Child: A Compassionate Look at Infertility*. Grand Rapids: Zondervan Publishing House, 1985.

Van Regenmorter, John and Sylvia and Joe S. McIlhaney, Jr. *Dear God, Why Can't We Have a Baby?* Grand Rapids: Baker Book House, 1986.

Coping with the Emotions of Infertility

Johnston, Patricia Irwin. *Understanding: A Guide to Impaired Fertility for Family and Friends*. Fort Wayne, Ind.: Perspectives Press, 1983.

Klug, Ronald. *How to Keep a Spiritual Journal*. Nashville: Thomas Nelson Publishers, 1982.

Landorf, Joyce. *The High Cost of Growing*. Nashville: Thomas Nelson Publishers, 1978.

Menning, Barbara Eck. *Infertility: A Guide for Childless Couples*. 2d ed. New York: Prentice-Hall, 1988.

Minirth, Frank B. *Happiness Is a Choice*. Grand Rapids: Baker Book House, 1978.

Pape, Dorothy R. *In Search of God's Ideal Woman*. Downers

Grove, Ill.: InterVarsity Press, 1976.

Salzer, Linda. *Infertility: How Couples Can Cope*. Boston: G. K. Hall and Co., 1986.

Marriage Enrichment

Clinebell, Howard J. and Charlotte H. *The Intimate Marriage*. New York: Harper and Row, 1970.

Dillow, Joseph. *Solomon on Sex*. Nashville: Thomas Nelson Publishers, 1977.

Mace, David R. *Close Companions*. New York: The Continuum Publishing Co., 1982.

Osborne, Cecil. *The Art of Understanding Your Mate*. Grand Rapids: Zondervan Publishing House, 1970.

Sell, Charles M. *Achieving the Impossible: Intimate Marriage*. Portland, Ore.: Multnomah Press, 1982.

Smalley, Gary. *If Only He Knew: A Valuable Guide to Knowing, Understanding and Loving Your Husband*. rev. ed. Grand Rapids: Zondervan Publishing House, 1982.

———. *For Better or For Best. A Valuable Guide to Knowing, Understanding and Loving Your Husband*. rev. ed. Grand Rapids: Zondervan Publishing House, 1982.

Wheat, Ed. *Love Life for Every Married Couple*. Grand Rapids: Zondervan Publishing House, 1980.

Childfree Living

Bombardieri, Merle. *The Baby Decision*. New York: Rawson, Wade Publishers, Inc., 1981.

Love, Vicky. *Childless is Not Less*. Minneapolis: Bethany House Publishers, 1984.

Peck, Ellen and Judith Senderowitz, eds. *Pronatalism: The Myth of Mom and Apple Pie*. New York: Thomas Y. Crowell Co., 1974.

Veevers, Jean E. *Childless by Choice*. Toronto: Butterworths, 1980.

Whelan, Elizabeth. *A Baby?* . . . *Maybe*. Indianapolis: Bobbs-Merrill Company, Inc., 1975.

Adoption

Johnston, Patricia Irwin. *An Adopter's Advocate*. Fort Wayne, Ind.: Perspectives Press, 1984.

Martin, Cynthia. *Beating the Adoption Game*. La Jolla, Calif.: Oak Tree Publications, 1980.

McNamara, Joan. *The Adoption Adviser*. New York: Hawthorn Books, Inc., 1975.

Plumez, Jacqueline Horner. *Successful Adoption*. New York: Harmony Books, 1982.

Prowledge, Fred. *The New Adoption Maze and How to Get Through It*. St. Louis: The C. V. Mosby Company, 1985.

Wishard, Laurie and William R. Wishard. *Adoption: The Grafted Tree*. San Francisco: Cragmont Publications, 1979.

Discussion of the Options

Andrews, Lori B. *New Conceptions*. New York: St. Martin's Press, 1984.

Mazor, Miriam and Harriet F. Simons, eds. *Infertility: Medical, Emotional and Social Considerations*. New York: Human Sciences Press, Inc., 1984.

McIlhaney, Joe S., Jr. and Susan Nethery. *1250 Health-Care Questions Women Ask*. Grand Rapids: Baker Book House, 1985.

Singer, Peter and Deane Wells. *The Reproduction Revolution*. New York: Oxford University Press, 1984.

Wood, Carl and Ann Westmore. *Test Tube Conception*. Englewood Cliffs, N.J.: Prentice-Hall, 1984.

Decision Making

Friesen, Garry and J. Robin Maxson. *Decision Making and the Will of God*. Portland, Ore.: Multnomah Press, 1980.

Gaither, Gloria. *Decisions*. Waco, Tex.: Word Books, 1982.

Prayer

Hallesby, O. *Prayer*. Minneapolis: Augsburg Press, 1931.

Knorr, Dandi Dailey. *When the Answer Is No*. Nashville: Broadman Press, 1985.

Lewis, C. S. *Letters to Malcolm: Chiefly on Prayer*. New York: Harcourt Brace Jovanovich, 1963, 1964.

Oates, Wayne. *Nurturing Silence in a Noisy Heart*. Garden City, N. Y.: Doubleday and Company, 1979.

ADDRESSES

Adoption

Families Adopting Children Everywhere (FACE)
Post Office Box 28058
Northwood Station
Baltimore, Maryland 21239

> *FACE is an adoptive parents support group which focuses on foreign and special needs adoptions. They also offer a bi-monthly newsletter.*

Holt International Children's Services
Post Office Box 2880
Eugene, Oregon 97402

> *Holt specializes in providing international adoptive services, especially for Korean children.*

Organization for a United Response (OURS), Inc.
3307 Highway 100 North, Suite 203
Minneapolis, Minnesota 55422

OURS *provides adoption information, the Helpline (a fam-
ily-to-family support system), and publishes a magazine six
times a year.*

General Information

American Fertility Society
2140 Eleventh Avenue South, Suite 200
Birmingham, Alabama 35205

AFS *provides up-to-date medical information on all aspects of
infertility.*

Perspectives Press (infertility and adoption publishers)
Post Office Box 90318
Indianapolis, Indiana 46290-0318

Support for Infertile Couples

RESOLVE
5 Water Street
Arlington, Massachusetts 02174

RESOLVE *is a nonprofit organization for the education and
support of infertile couples.*

Stepping Stones
2900 North Rock Road
Wichita, Kansas 67226

Stepping Stones *is a newsletter published bimonthly for the
encouragement and support of infertile Christian couples.*

Note: Addresses change over time, but current addresses of
many organizations can be found in the *Encyclopedia of Associations* at most libraries.